Ann Leight
10/23/96

The Essential Rumi

A Beginning

The Essential Rumi ✌

Translated by COLEMAN BARKS

    with JOHN MOYNE

        A. J. ARBERRY

        REYNOLD NICHOLSON

📖 HarperSanFrancisco

A Division of HarperCollins*Publishers*

for the compassionate heart within the mind, the light

within the body,

for the sun, Shams of Tabriz, and Bawa Muhaiyaddeen

Book design by Jaime Robles.
Set in Sabon type with Fournier ornaments.

Library of Congress Cataloging-in-Publication Data
Jalāl al-Dīn Rūmī, Maulana
  [Selections. English. 1994]
  The essential Rumi / translated by Coleman Barks, with John Moyne,
A. J. Arberry, Reynold Nicholson.
    p.   cm.
  Includes index.
  ISBN 0–06–250958–6 (cloth: alk. paper)
  ISBN 0–06–250959–4 (pbk.: alk. paper)
  1. Jalāl al-Dīn Rūmī, Maulana, 1207–1273—Translations into English.
2. Sufi poetry, Persian—Translations into English.   I. Barks, Coleman.
II. Title.
  PK6480.E5.B37 1995
  891'.5511–dc20
  [B]   94–44995
                                          CIP

  96   97   98   99   ❖   HAD   10   9

~ Contents

✍ On Rumi

Persians and Afghanis call Rumi "Jelaluddin Balkhi." He was born September 30, 1207, in Balkh, Afghanistan, which was then part of the Persian empire. The name *Rumi* means "from Roman Anatolia." He was not known by that name, of course, until after his family, fleeing the threat of the invading Mongol armies, emigrated to Konya, Turkey, sometime between 1215 and 1220. His father, Bahauddin Walad, was a theologian and jurist and a mystic of uncertain lineage. Bahauddin Walad's *Maarif,* a collection of notes, diarylike remarks, sermons, and strange accounts of visionary experiences, has shocked most of the conventional scholars who have tried to understand them. He shows a startlingly sensual freedom in stating his union with God. Rumi was instructed in his father's secret inner life by a former student of his father, Burhanuddin Mahaqqiq. Burhan and Rumi also studied Sanai and Attar. At his father's death Rumi took over the position of sheikh in the dervish learning community in Konya. His life seems to have been a fairly normal one for a religious scholar—teaching, meditating, helping the poor—until in the late fall of 1244 when he met a stranger who put a question to him. That stranger was the wandering dervish, Shams of Tabriz, who had traveled throughout the Middle East searching and praying for someone who could "endure my company." A voice came, "What will you give in return?" "My head!" "The one you seek is Jelaluddin of Konya."

The question Shams spoke made the learned professor faint to the ground. We cannot be entirely certain of the question, but according to the most reliable account Shams asked who was greater, Muhammad or Bestami, for Bestami had said, "How great is my glory," whereas Muhammad had acknowledged in his prayer to God, "We do not know You as we should."

Rumi heard the depth out of which the question came and fell to the ground. He was finally able to answer that Muhammad was greater, because Bestami had taken one gulp of the divine and stopped there, whereas for Muhammad the way was always unfolding. There are various versions of this encounter, but whatever the facts, Shams and Rumi became inseparable. Their Friendship is one of the mysteries. They spent months together without any human needs, transported into a region of pure conversation. This ecstatic connection caused difficulties in the religious community. Rumi's students felt neglected. Sensing the trouble, Shams disappeared as suddenly as he had appeared. Annemarie Schimmel, a scholar immersed for forty years in the works of Rumi, thinks that it was at this first disappearance that Rumi began the transformation into a mystical artist. "He turned into a poet, began to listen to music, and sang, whirling around, hour after hour."

Word came that Shams was in Damascus. Rumi sent his son, Sultan Velad, to Syria to bring his Friend back to Konya. When Rumi and Shams met for the second time, they fell at each other's feet, so that "no one knew who was lover and who the beloved." Shams stayed in Rumi's home and was married to a young girl who had been brought up in the family. Again the long mystical conversation (*sohbet*) began, and again the jealousies grew.

On the night of December 5, 1248, as Rumi and Shams were talking, Shams was called to the back door. He went out, never to be seen again. Most likely, he was murdered with the connivance of Rumi's son, Allaedin; if so, Shams indeed gave his head for the privilege of mystical Friendship.

The mystery of the Friend's absence covered Rumi's world. He himself went out searching for Shams and journeyed again to Damascus. It was there that he realized,

> Why should I seek? I am the same as
> he. His essence speaks through me.
> I have been looking for myself!

The union became complete. There was full *fana*, annihilation in the Friend. Shams was writing the poems. Rumi called the huge collection of his odes and quatrains *The Works of Shams of Tabriz*.

After Shams's death and Rumi's merging with him, another companion was found, Saladin Zarkub, the goldsmith. Saladin became the Friend to whom Rumi addressed his poems, not so fierily as to Shams, but with quiet tenderness. When Saladin died, Husam Chelebi, Rumi's scribe and favorite student, assumed this role. Rumi claimed that Husam was the source, the one who understood the vast, secret order of the *Mathnawi*, that great work that shifts so fantastically from theory to folklore to jokes to ecstatic poetry. For the last twelve years of his life, Rumi dictated the six volumes of this masterwork to Husam. He died on December 17, 1273.

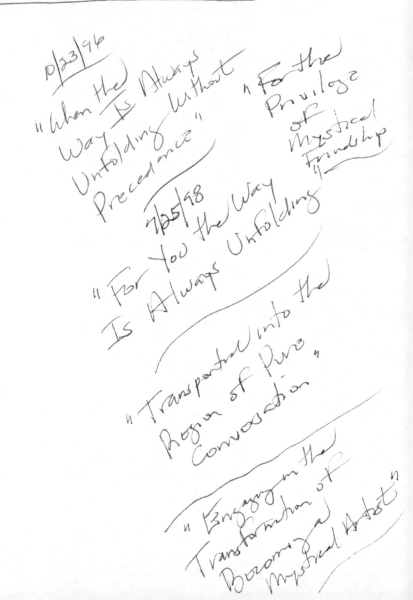

10/23/96

"When the Way Is Always Unfolding Without Precedence"

"For the Privilege of Mystical Friendship"

7/25/98

"For You the Way Is Always Unfolding"

"Transported into the Region of Pure Convocation"

"Engaging in the Transformation of Becoming a Mystical Artist"

" Living out of
a Fluid,
Continuously Self-
Revising, Self-
Interrupting Medium
Spoken From
Within Something "
7/25/98

⤳ A Note on the Organization of This Book

1·0/23/96

The design of this book is meant to confuse scholars who would divide Rumi's poetry into the accepted categories: the quatrains (*rubaiyat*) and odes (*ghazals*) of the *Divan*, the six books of the *Mathnawi*, the discourses, the letters, and the almost unknown *Six Sermons*. The mind wants categories, but Rumi's creativity was a continuous fountaining from beyond forms and the mind, or as the sufis say, from a mind within the mind, the *qalb*, which is a great compassionate generosity.

The twenty-seven divisions here are faint and playful palimpsests spread over Rumi's imagination. Poems easily splash over, slide from one overlay to another. The unity behind *La'illaha il'Allahu* ("there's no reality but God; there is only God"), is the one substance the other subheadings float within at various depths. If one actually selected an "essential" Rumi, it would be the *zikr*, the remembering that everything is God. Likewise, the titles of the poems are whimsical. Rumi's individual poems in Persian have no titles. His collection of quatrains and odes is called *The Works of Shams of Tabriz* (*Divani Shamsi Tabriz*). The six books of poetry he dictated to his scribe, Husam Chelebi, are simply titled *Spiritual Couplets* (*Mathnawi*), or sometimes he refers to them as *The Book of Husam*. The wonderfully goofy title of the discourses, *In It What's in It* (*Fihi Ma Fihi*), may mean "what's in the *Mathnawi* is in this too," or it may be the kind of hands-thrown-up gesture it sounds like.

All of which makes the point that these poems are not monumental in the Western sense of memorializing moments; they are not discrete entities but a fluid, continuously self-revising, self-interrupting medium. They are not so much *about* anything as spoken from *within* something. Call it enlightenment, ecstatic love, spirit, soul, truth, the ocean of *ilm* (divine luminous wisdom), or the covenant of *alast* (the original agreement with God). Names do not matter. Some resonance of ocean resides in everyone. Rumi's poetry can be felt as a salt breeze from that, traveling inland.

These poems were created, not in packets and batches of art, but as part of a constant, practical, and mysterious discourse Rumi was having with a dervish learning community. The focus changed from stern to ecstatic, from everyday to esoteric, as the needs of the group arose. Poetry and music and movement were parts of that communal and secretly individual work of opening hearts and exploring the mystery of union with the divine. The form of this collection means to honor the variety and simultaneity of that mystical union.

Most of the facts, dates, and chew-toys for the intellect are stashed in the Notes.

Rumi puts a prose prayer at the beginning of each book of the *Mathnawi*. Here's the blessing he gives before Book IV.

Praise to Early-Waking Grievers

In the name of God the Most Merciful, and the Most Compassionate.

This is the fourth journey toward home, toward where the great advantages are waiting for us. Reading it, mystics will feel very happy, as a meadow feels when it hears thunder, the good news of rain coming, as tired eyes look forward to sleeping. Joy for the spirit, health for the body. In here is what genuine devotion wants, refreshment, sweet fruit ripe enough for the pickiest picker, medicine, detailed directions on how to get to the Friend. All praise to God. Here is the way to renew connection with your soul, and rest from difficulties. The study of this book will be painful to those who feel separate from God. It will make the others grateful. In the hold of this ship is a cargo not found in the attractiveness of young women. Here is a reward for lovers of God. A full moon and an inheritance you thought you had lost are now returned to you. More hope for the hopeful, lucky finds for foragers, wonderful things thought of to do. Anticipation after depression, expanding after contraction. The sun comes out, and that light is what we give, in this book, to our spiritual descendants. Our gratitude to God holds them to us, and brings more besides. As the Andalusian poet, Adi al-Riga, says,

I was sleeping, and being comforted
by a cool breeze, when suddenly a gray dove
from a thicket sang and sobbed with longing,
and reminded me of my own passion.

I had been away from my own soul so long,
so late-sleeping, but that dove's crying
woke me and made me cry. *Praise*
to all early-waking grievers!

Some go first, and others come long afterward. God blesses both and
all in the line, and replaces what has been consumed, and provides for
those who work the soil of helpfulness, and blesses Muhammad and
Jesus and every other messenger and prophet. Amen, and may the
Lord of all created beings bless you.

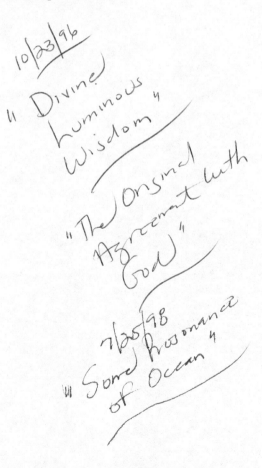

1 ↝ The Tavern:

Whoever Brought Me Here Will Have to Take Me Home

[handwritten: " A Core Breaking Apart "]

[handwritten: 7/25/98]

ON THE TAVERN

In the tavern are many wines—the wine of delight in color and form and taste, the wine of the intellect's agility, the fine port of stories, and the cabernet of soul singing. Being human means entering this place where entrancing varieties of desire are served. The grapeskin of ego breaks and a pouring begins. Fermentation is one of the oldest symbols for human transformation. When grapes combine their juice and are closed up together for a time in a dark place, the results are spectacular. This is what lets two drunks meet so that they don't know who is who. Pronouns no longer apply in the tavern's mud-world of excited confusion and half-articulated wantings.

But after some time in the tavern, a point comes, a memory of elsewhere, a longing for the source, and the drunks must set off from the tavern and begin the return. The Qur'an says, "We are all returning." The tavern is a kind of glorious hell that human beings enjoy and suffer and then push off from in their search for truth. The tavern is a dangerous region where sometimes disguises are necessary, but never hide your heart, Rumi urges. Keep open there. A breaking apart, a crying out into the street, begins in the tavern, and the human soul turns to find its way home.

It's 4 A.M. Nasruddin leaves the tavern and walks the town aimlessly. A policeman stops him. "Why are you out wandering the streets in the middle of the night?" "Sir," replies Nasruddin, "if I knew the answer to that question, I would have been home hours ago!"

WHO SAYS WORDS WITH MY MOUTH?

All day I think about it, then at night I say it.
Where did I come from, and what am I supposed to be doing?
I have no idea.
My soul is from elsewhere, I'm sure of that,
and I intend to end up there.

This drunkenness began in some other tavern.
When I get back around to that place,
I'll be completely sober. Meanwhile,
I'm like a bird from another continent, sitting in this aviary.
The day is coming when I fly off,
but who is it now in my ear who hears my voice?
Who says words with my mouth?

Who looks out with my eyes? What is the soul?
I cannot stop asking.
If I could taste one sip of an answer,
I could break out of this prison for drunks.
I didn't come here of my own accord, and I can't leave that way.
Whoever brought me here will have to take me home.

This poetry. I never know what I'm going to say.
I don't plan it.
When I'm outside the saying of it,
I get very quiet and rarely speak at all.

7/25/98

———

We have a huge barrel of wine, but no cups.
That's fine with us. Every morning
we glow and in the evening we glow again.

They say there's no future for us. They're right.
Which is fine with us.

———

A COMMUNITY OF THE SPIRIT

There is a community of the spirit.
Join it, and feel the delight
of walking in the noisy street,
and *being* the noise.

Drink *all* your passion,
and be a disgrace.

Close both eyes
to see with the other eye.

Open your hands,
if you want to be held.

Sit down in this circle.

Quit acting like a wolf, and feel
the shepherd's love filling you.

At night, your beloved wanders.
Don't accept consolations.

Close your mouth against food.
Taste the lover's mouth in yours.

You moan, "She left me." "He left me."
Twenty more will come.

Be empty of worrying.
Think of who created thought!

Why do you stay in prison   7/25/98
when the door is so wide open?

Move outside the tangle of fear-thinking.
Live in silence.

Flow down and down in always
widening rings of being.

There's a strange frenzy in my head,
of birds flying,
each particle circulating on its own.
Is the one I love *everywhere?*

🖎

Drunks fear the police,
but the police are drunk too.

People in this town love them both
like different chess pieces.

🖎

A CHILDREN'S GAME

Listen to the poet Sanai,
who lived secluded: "Don't wander out on the road
in your ecstasy. Sleep in the tavern."

When a drunk strays out to the street,
children make fun of him.
                          He falls down in the mud.
He takes any and every road.
                          The children follow,
not knowing the taste of wine, or how
his drunkenness feels. All people on the planet
are children, except for a very few.
No one is grown up except those free of desire.

God said,
          "The world is a play, a children's game,
and you are the children."
                          God speaks the truth.
If you haven't left the child's play,
how can you be an adult?
                          Without purity of spirit,
if you're still in the middle of lust and greed

and other wantings, you're like children
playing at sexual intercourse.
                              They wrestle
and rub together, but it's not sex!

The same with the fightings of mankind.
It's a squabble with play-swords.
No purpose, totally futile.

Like kids on hobby horses, soldiers claim to be riding
Boraq, Muhammad's night-horse, or Duldul, his mule.

Your actions mean nothing, the sex and war that you do.
You're holding part of your pants and prancing around,
Dun-da-dun, dun-da-dun.

Don't wait till you die to see this.
Recognize that your imagination and your thinking
and your sense perception are reed canes
that children cut and pretend are horsies.

The knowing of mystic lovers is different.
The empirical, sensory, sciences
are like a donkey loaded with books,
or like the makeup woman's makeup.
                                        It washes off.
But if you lift the baggage rightly, it will give joy.
Don't carry your knowledge-load for some selfish reason.
Deny your desires and willfulness,
and a real mount may appear under you.

Don't be satisfied with the *name* of HU,
with just words about it.

Experience *that breathing*.
From books and words come fantasy,
and sometimes, from fantasy comes union.

Gone, inner and outer,
no moon, no ground or sky.

5

Don't hand me another glass of wine.
Pour it in my mouth.
I've lost the way to my mouth.

❧

The wine we really drink is our own blood.
Our bodies ferment in these barrels.
We give everything for a glass of this.
We give our minds for a sip.

❧

THE MANY WINES

God has given us a dark wine so potent that,
drinking it, we leave the two worlds.

God has put into the form of hashish a power
to deliver the taster from self-consciousness.

God has made sleep so
that it erases every thought.

God made Majnun love Layla so much that
just her dog would cause confusion in him.

There are thousands of wines
that can take over our minds.

Don't think all ecstasies
are the same!

Jesus was lost in his love for God.
His donkey was drunk with barley.

Drink from the presence of saints,
not from those other jars.

Every object, every being,
is a jar full of delight.

Be a connoisseur,
and taste with caution.

7/25/98

Any wine will get you high.
Judge like a king, and choose the purest,

the ones unadulterated with fear,
or some urgency about "what's needed."

Drink the wine that moves you
as a camel moves when it's been untied,
and is just ambling about.

SPECIAL PLATES

Notice how each particle moves.
Notice how everyone has just arrived here
            from a journey.
Notice how each wants a different food.
Notice how the stars vanish as the sun comes up,
            and how all streams stream toward the ocean.

Look at the chefs preparing special plates
            for everyone, according to what they need.
Look at this cup that can hold the ocean.
Look at those who see the face.
Look through Shams' eyes
            into the water that is
            entirely jewels.

BURNT KABOB

Last year, I admired wines. This,
I'm wandering inside the red world.

Last year, I gazed at the fire.
This year I'm burnt kabob.

Thirst drove me down to the water
where I drank the moon's reflection.

Now I am a lion staring up totally
lost in love with the thing itself.

Don't ask questions about longing.
Look in my face.

Soul drunk, body ruined, these two
sit helpless in a wrecked wagon.
Neither knows how to fix it.

And my heart, I'd say it was more
like a donkey sunk in a mudhole,
struggling and miring deeper.

But listen to me: for one moment,
quit being sad. Hear blessings
dropping their blossoms
around you. God.

THE NEW RULE

It's the old rule that drunks have to argue
and get into fights.
The lover is just as bad. He falls into a hole.
But down in that hole he finds something shining,
worth more than any amount of money or power.

Last night the moon came dropping its clothes in the street.
I took it as a sign to start singing,
falling up into the bowl of sky.
The bowl breaks. Everywhere is falling everywhere.
Nothing else to do.

Here's the new rule: break the wineglass,
and fall toward the glassblower's breath.

This that is tormented and very tired,
tortured with restraints like a madman,
this heart.
            Still you keep breaking the shell
to get the taste of its kernel!

2 ✌ Bewilderment:
I Have Five Things to Say

ON BEWILDERMENT

At the verge of full fana *(annihilation in God) there seems to be a region of sweet confusion, the sense of being in many places at once saying multiple sentences. A hazy melting, fragile and nearly blank. Profound ignorance within which conventional, calm behavior seems* insane!

Rumi's poems are not well-trimmed, Persian miniature gardens. They are more like, as scholar Annemarie Schimmel says, the paintings in the Turkoman style—full of abrupt movement, odd flowers and bushes, demons and talking animals.

I HAVE FIVE THINGS TO SAY

The wakened lover speaks directly to the beloved,
"You are the sky my spirit circles in,
the love inside love, the resurrection-place.

Let this window be your ear.
I have lost consciousness many times
with longing for your listening silence,
and your life-quickening smile.

You give attention to the smallest matters,
my suspicious doubts, and to the greatest.

You know my coins are counterfeit,
but you accept them anyway,
my impudence and my pretending!

I have five things to say,
five fingers to give
into your grace.

First, when I was apart from you,
        this world did not exist,
            nor any other.

Second, whatever I was looking for
        was always you.

Third, why did I ever learn to count to three?

Fourth, my cornfield is burning!

Fifth, this finger stands for Rabia,
        and this is for someone else.
            Is there a difference?

Are these words or tears?
Is weeping speech?
What shall I do, my love?"

So he speaks, and everyone around
begins to cry with him, laughing crazily,
moaning in the spreading union
of lover and beloved.

This is the true religion. All others
are thrown-away bandages beside it.

This is the *sema* of slavery and mastery
dancing together. This is not-being.

Neither words, nor any natural fact
can express this.

I know these dancers.
Day and night I sing their songs
in this phenomenal cage.

My soul, don't try to answer now!
Find a friend, and hide.

But what can stay hidden?
Love's secret is always lifting its head
out from under the covers,
"Here I am!"

ACTS OF HELPLESSNESS

Here are the miracle-signs you want: that
you cry through the night and get up at dawn, asking,
that in the absence of what you ask for your day gets dark,
your neck thin as a spindle, that what you give away
is all you own, that you sacrifice belongings,
sleep, health, your head, that you often
sit down in a fire like aloes wood, and often go out
to meet a blade like a battered helmet.

When acts of helplessness become habitual,
those are the *signs*.

But you run back and forth listening for unusual events,
peering into the faces of travelers.
"Why are you looking at me like a madman?"
I have lost a friend. Please forgive me.

Searching like that does not fail.
There will come a rider who holds you close.
You faint and gibber. The uninitiated say, "He's faking."
How could they know?
Water washes over a beached fish, the water
of those signs I just mentioned.

Excuse my wandering.
How can one be orderly with this?
It's like counting leaves in a garden,
along with the song-notes of partridges,
and crows.
                    Sometimes organization
and computation become absurd.

7/25/98

Of these two thousand "I" and "We" people,
which am I?

Don't try to keep me from asking!
Listen, when I'm this out of control!
But don't put anything breakable in my way!

There is an original inside me.
What's here is a mirror for that, for you.

If you are joyful, I am.
If you grieve, or if you're bitter, or graceful,
I take on those qualities.

Like the shadow of a cypress tree in the meadow,
like the shadow of a rose, I live
close to the rose.

If I separated myself from you,
I would turn entirely thorn.

Every second, I drink another cup of my own blood-wine.
Every instant, I break an empty cup against your door.

I reach out, wanting you to tear me open.

Saladin's generosity lights a candle in my chest.
Who *am* I then?
His empty begging bowl.

હ

Late, by myself, in the boat of myself,
no light and no land anywhere,
cloudcover thick. I try to stay
just above the surface, yet I'm already under
and living within the ocean.

હ

Does sunset sometimes look like the sun's coming up?
Do you know what a faithful love is like?

You're crying. You say you've burned yourself.
But can you think of anyone who's not
hazy with smoke?

BE MELTING SNOW

Totally conscious, and apropos of nothing, you come to see me.
Is someone here? I ask.
The moon. The full moon is inside your house.

My friends and I go running out into the street.
I'm in here, comes a voice from the house, but we aren't listening.
We're looking up at the sky.
My pet nightingale sobs like a drunk in the garden.
Ringdoves scatter with small cries, *Where, Where.*
It's midnight. The whole neighborhood is up and out
in the street thinking, *The cat burglar has come back.*
The actual thief is there too, saying out loud,
Yes, the cat burglar is somewhere in this crowd.
No one pays attention.

Lo, I am with you always means when you look for God,
God is in the look of your eyes,
in the thought of looking, nearer to you than your self,
or things that have happened to you
There's no need to go outside.

7/25/98

Be melting snow.
Wash yourself of yourself.

A white flower grows in the quietness.
Let your tongue become that flower.

I need a mouth as wide as the sky
to say the nature of a True Person, language
as large as longing.

The fragile vial inside me often breaks.
No wonder I go mad and disappear for three days
every month with the moon.

For anyone in love with you,
it's always these invisible days.

I've lost the thread of the story I was telling.
My elephant roams his dream of Hindustan again.
Narrative, poetics, destroyed, my body,
a dissolving, a return.

Friend, I've shrunk to a hair trying to say your story.
Would you tell mine?
I've made up so many love stories.
Now I feel fictional.
Tell *me!*
The truth is, you are speaking, not me.
I am Sinai, and you are Moses walking there.
This poetry is an echo of what you say.
A piece of land can't speak, or know anything!
Or if it can, only within limits.

The body is a device to calculate
the astronomy of the spirit.
Look through that astrolabe
and become oceanic.

Why this distracted talk?
It's not my fault I rave.
You did this.
Do you approve of my love-madness?

Say yes.
What language will you say it in, Arabic or Persian,
or what? Once again, I must be tied up.

Bring the curly ropes of your hair.

                      Now I remember the story.

A True Man stares at his old shoes
and sheepskin jacket. Every day he goes up
to his attic to look at his work-shoes and worn-out coat.
This is his wisdom, to remember the original clay
and not get drunk with ego and arrogance.

To visit those shoes and jacket
is praise.

The Absolute works with nothing.
The workshop, the materials
are what does not exist.

Try and be a sheet of paper with nothing on it.
Be a spot of ground where nothing is growing,
where something might be planted,
a seed, possibly, from the Absolute.

WHERE ARE WE?

An invisible bird flies over,
but casts a quick shadow.

What is the body? That shadow of a shadow
of your love, that somehow contains
the entire universe.

A man sleeps heavily,
though something blazes in him like the sun,
like a magnificent fringe sewn up under the hem.

He turns under the covers.
Any image is a lie:

    A clear red stone tastes sweet.

    You kiss a beautiful mouth, and a key
    turns in the lock of your fear.

A spoken sentence sharpens to a fine edge.

A mother dove looks for her nest,
asking where, *ku?* Where, *ku?*

Where the lion lies down.
Where any man or woman goes to cry.
Where the sick go when they hope to get well.

Where a wind lifts that helps with winnowing,
and, the same moment, sends a ship on its way.

Where anyone says *Only God Is Real.*
Ya Hu! Where beyond *where.*

A bright weaver's shuttle flashes back and forth,
east-west, *Where-are-we? Ma ku? Maku.*
like the sun saying *Where are we?*
as it weaves with the asking.

❧

The Friend comes into my body
looking for the center, unable
to find it, draws a blade,
strikes anywhere.

❧

There is a light seed grain inside.
You fill it with yourself, or it dies.

I'm caught in this curling energy! Your hair!
Whoever's calm and sensible is insane!

❧

Do you think I know what I'm doing?
That for one breath or half-breath I belong to myself?
As much as a pen knows what it's writing,
or the ball can guess where it's going next.

3 ~ Emptiness and Silence: The Night Air

[handwritten: 7/25/98 "Where's the Inner Story? Where's the Unfolding? What's the Unfolding? Compose Compose Compose From Silence" RL]

[handwritten: 10/23/96]

ON SILENCE

In Persian poetry the poet often refers to himself or herself by name at the end of a poem as a sort of signature. Rumi's variation on this is to refer instead to Shams (over a thousand poems end this way) or to silence. He gives the poetry to its true authorship, including the *[handwritten: 7/25/98]* *emptiness* after *as part of the poem. Five hundred odes conclude with* khamush, *silence. Rumi is less interested in language, more attuned to the sources of it. He keeps asking Husam, "Who's making this music?" He sometimes gives the wording over to the invisible flute player: "Let that musician finish this poem." Words are not important in themselves, but as resonators for a center. Rumi has a whole theory of language based on the reed flute* (ney). *Beneath everything we say, and within each note of the reed flute, lies a nostalgia for the reed bed. Language and music are possible only because we're empty, hollow, and separated from the source. All language is a longing for home. Why is there not a second tonality, he muses, a note in praise of the craftsman's skill, which fashioned the bare cylinder into a* ney, *the intricate human form with its nine holes?*

[handwritten: 7/25/98 "Words Are Resonance for a Center from a Center" RL]

THE REED FLUTE'S SONG

Listen to the story told by the reed,
of being separated.

"Since I was cut from the reedbed,
I have made this crying sound.

Anyone apart from someone he loves
understands what I say.

Anyone pulled from a source
longs to go back.

At any gathering I am there,
mingling in the laughing and grieving,

a friend to each, but few
will hear the secrets hidden

within the notes. No ears for that.
Body flowing out of spirit,

spirit up from body: no concealing
that mixing. But it's not given us

to *see* the soul. The reed flute
is fire, not wind. Be that empty."

Hear the love fire tangled
in the reed notes, as bewilderment

melts into wine. The reed is a friend
to all who want the fabric torn

and drawn away. The reed is hurt
and salve combining. Intimacy

and longing for intimacy, one
song. A disastrous surrender

and a fine love, together. The one
who secretly hears this is senseless.

A tongue has one customer, the ear.
A sugarcane flute has such effect

because it was able to make sugar
in the reedbed. The sound it makes

is for everyone. Days full of wanting,
let them go by without worrying

that they do. Stay where you are
inside such a pure, hollow note.

Every thirst gets satisfied except
that of these fish, the mystics,

who swim a vast ocean of grace
still somehow longing for it!

No one lives in that without
being nourished every day.

But if someone doesn't want to hear
the song of the reed flute,

it's best to cut conversation
short, say good-bye, and leave.

A THIRSTY FISH

I don't get tired of you. Don't grow weary
of being compassionate toward me!

All this thirst equipment
must surely be *tired* of me,
the waterjar, the water carrier.

I have a thirsty fish in me
that can never find enough
of what it's thirsty for!

Show me the way to the ocean!
Break these half-measures,
these small containers.

All this fantasy
and grief.

Let my house be drowned in the wave
that rose last night out of the courtyard
hidden in the center of my chest.

Joseph fell like the moon into my well.
The harvest I expected was washed away.
But no matter.

A fire has risen above my tombstone hat.
I don't want learning, or dignity,
or respectability.

I want this music and this dawn
and the warmth of your cheek against mine.

The grief-armies assemble,
but I'm not going with them.

This is how it always is
when I finish a poem.

A great silence overcomes me,
and I wonder why I ever thought
to use language.

ENOUGH WORDS?

How does a part of the world leave the world?
How can wetness leave water?

Don't try to put out a fire
by throwing on more fire!
Don't wash a wound with blood!

No matter how fast you run,
your shadow more than keeps up.
Sometimes, it's in front!

Only full, overhead sun
diminishes your shadow.

But that shadow has been serving you!
What hurts you, blesses you.
Darkness is your candle.
Your boundaries are your quest.

I can explain this, but it would break
the glass cover on your heart,
and there's no fixing that.

You must have shadow and light source both.
Listen, and lay your head under the tree of awe.

When from that tree, feathers and wings sprout
on you, be quieter than a dove.
Don't open your mouth for even a *cooooooo*.

When a frog slips into the water, the snake
cannot get it. Then the frog climbs back out
and croaks, and the snake moves toward him again.

Even if the frog learned to hiss, still the snake
would hear through the hiss the information
he needed, the frog voice underneath.

But if the frog could be completely silent,
then the snake would go back to sleeping,
and the frog could reach the barley.

The soul lives there in the silent breath.

And that grain of barley is such that,
when you put it in the ground,
it grows.
            Are these enough words,
or shall I squeeze more juice from this?
Who am I, my friend?

THIS WORLD WHICH IS MADE OF
OUR LOVE FOR EMPTINESS

Praise to the emptiness that blanks out existence. Existence:
this place made from our love for that emptiness!
Yet somehow comes emptiness,
this existence goes.
Praise to that happening, over and over!

For years I pulled my own existence out of emptiness.
Then one swoop, one swing of the arm,
that work is over.
Free of who I was, free of presence, free of
dangerous fear, hope,
free of mountainous wanting.

The here-and-now mountain is a tiny piece of a piece
of straw
blown off into emptiness.

These words I'm saying so much begin to lose meaning:
existence, emptiness, mountain, straw: words
and what they try to say swept
out the window, down the slant of the roof.

QUIETNESS

Inside this new love, die.
Your way begins on the other side.
Become the sky.
Take an axe to the prison wall.
Escape.
Walk out like someone suddenly born into color.
Do it now.
You're covered with thick cloud.
Slide out the side. Die,
and be quiet. Quietness is the surest sign
that you've died.
Your old life was a frantic running
from silence.

The speechless full moon
comes out now.

SANAI

Someone says, *Sanai is dead.*
No small thing to say.

He was not bits of husk,
or a puddle that freezes overnight,
or a comb that cracks when you use it,
or a pod crushed open on the ground.

He was fine powder in a rough clay dish.
He knew what both worlds were worth:
A grain of barley.

One he slung down, the other up.

The inner soul, that presence of which most know nothing,
about which poets are so ambiguous,
he married that one to the beloved.

His pure gold wine pours on the thick wine dregs.
They mix and rise and separate again
to meet down the road. Dear friend from Marghaz,
who lived in Rayy, in Rum, Kurd from the mountains,
each of us returns home.

Silk must not be compared with striped canvas.

Be quiet and clear now
like the final touchpoints of calligraphy.

Your name has been erased
from the roaring volume of speech.

A JUST-FINISHING CANDLE

A candle is made to become entirely flame.
In that annihilating moment
it has no shadow.

It is nothing but a tongue of light
describing a refuge.

Look at this
just-finishing candle stub
as someone who is finally safe
from virtue and vice,

the pride and the shame
we claim from those.

I've said before that every craftsman
searches for what's not there
to practice his craft.

A builder looks for the rotten hole
where the roof caved in. A water carrier
picks the empty pot. A carpenter
stops at the house with no door.

Workers rush toward some hint
of emptiness, which they then
start to fill. Their hope, though,
is for emptiness, so don't think
you must avoid it. It contains
what you need!
        Dear soul, if you were not friends
with the vast nothing inside,
why would you always be casting your net
into it, and waiting so patiently?

This invisible ocean has given you such abundance,
but still you call it "death,"
that which provides you sustenance and work.

God has allowed some magical reversal to occur,
so that you see the scorpion pit
as an object of desire,
and all the beautiful expanse around it
as dangerous and swarming with snakes.

This is how strange your fear of death
and emptiness is, and how perverse
the attachment to what you want.

Now that you've heard me
on your misapprehensions, dear friend,
listen to Attar's story on the same subject.

He strung the pearls of this
about King Mahmud, how among the spoils
of his Indian campaign there was a Hindu boy,

whom he adopted as a son. He educated
and provided royally for the boy
and later made him vice-regent, seated
on a gold throne beside himself.

One day he found the young man weeping.
"Why are you crying? You're the companion
of an emperor! The entire nation is ranged out
before you like stars that you can command!"

The young man replied, "I am remembering
my mother and my father, and how they
scared me as a child with threats of you!
'Uh-oh, he's headed for King Mahmud's court!
Nothing could be more hellish!' Where are they now
when they should see me sitting here?"

This incident is about your fear of changing.
You are the Hindu boy. *Mahmud,* which means,
Praise to the End, is the spirit's
poverty, or emptiness.

The mother and father are your attachment
to beliefs and bloodties
and desires and comforting habits.

Don't listen to them!
They seem to protect,
but they imprison.

They are your worst enemies.
They make you afraid
of living in emptiness.

Some day you'll weep tears of delight in that court,
remembering your mistaken parents!

Know that your body nurtures the spirit,
helps it grow, and then gives it wrong advice.

The body becomes, eventually, like a vest
of chainmail in peaceful years,
too hot in summer and too cold in winter.

But the body's desires, in another way, are like
an unpredictable associate, whom you must be
patient with. And that companion is helpful,
because patience expands your capacity
to love and feel peace.

The patience of a rose close to a thorn
keeps it fragrant. It's patience that gives milk
to the male camel still nursing in its third year,
and patience is what the prophets show to us.

The beauty of careful sewing on a shirt
is the patience it contains.

Friendship and loyalty have patience
as the strength of their connections.

Feeling lonely and ignoble indicates
that you haven't been patient.

Be with those who mix with God
as honey blends with milk, and say,

"Anything that comes and goes,
rises and sets,
is not what I love."

Live in the one who created the prophets,
else you'll be like a caravan fire left
to flare itself out alone beside the road.

EMPTINESS

Consider the difference
in our actions and God's actions.

We often ask, "Why did you do that?"
or "Why did I act like that?"

We do act, and yet everything we do
is God's creative action.

We look back and analyze the events
of our lives, but there is another way
of seeing, a backward-and-forward-at-once
vision, that is not rationally understandable.

Only God can understand it.
Satan made the excuse, *You caused me to fall,*
whereas Adam said to God, *We did this
to ourselves.* After this repentance,
God asked Adam, *Since all is within
my foreknowledge, why didn't you
defend yourself with that reason?*

Adam answered, *I was afraid,
and I wanted to be reverent.*

Whoever acts with respect will get respect.
Whoever brings sweetness will be served almond cake.
Good women are drawn to be with good men.

Honor your friend.
Or treat him rudely,
and see what happens!

Love, tell an incident now
that will clarify this mystery
of how we act freely, and are yet
compelled. One hand shakes with palsy.
Another shakes because you slapped it away.

Both tremblings come from God,
but you feel guilty for the one,
and what about the other?

These are intellectual questions.
The spirit approaches the matter
differently. Omar once had a friend, a scientist,
Bu'l-Hakam, who was flawless at solving
empirical problems, but he could not follow Omar
into the area of illumination and wonder.

Now I return to the text, "And He is with you,
wherever you are," but when have I ever left it!

Ignorance is God's prison.
Knowing is God's palace.

We sleep in God's unconsciousness.
We wake in God's open hand.

We weep God's rain.
We laugh God's lightning.

Fighting and peacefulness
both take place within God.

Who are we then
in this complicated world-tangle,
that is really just the single, straight
line down at the beginning of *ALLAH*?

Nothing.
We are
emptiness.

✍

When you are with everyone but me,
                              you're with no one.
When you are with no one but me,
                              you're with everyone.

Instead of being so bound up *with* everyone,
                              be everyone.
When you become that many, you're nothing.
                              Empty.

✍

NO FLAG

I used to want buyers for my words.
Now I wish someone would buy me away from words.

I've made a lot of charmingly profound images,
scenes with Abraham, and Abraham's father, Azar,
who was also famous for icons.

I'm so tired of what I've been doing.

Then one image without form came,
and I quit.

Look for someone else to tend the shop.
I'm out of the image-making business.

Finally I know the freedom
of madness.

A random image arrives. I scream,
"Get out!" It disintegrates.

Only love.
Only the holder the flag fits into,
and wind. No flag.

THE FOOD SACK

One day a sufi sees an empty food sack hanging on a nail.
He begins to turn and tear his shirt, saying,
Food for what needs no food!
A cure for hunger!

His burning grows and others join him,
shouting and moaning in the love-fire.

An idle passerby comments, "It's only an empty sack."

The sufi says, *Leave. You want what we do not want.*
You are not a lover.

A lover's food is the love of bread,
not the bread. No one who really loves,
loves existence.

Lovers have nothing to do with existence.
They collect the interest without the capital.

No wings, yet they fly all over the world. No hands,
but they carry the polo ball from the field.

That dervish got a sniff of reality.
Now he weaves baskets of pure vision.

Lovers pitch tents on a field of nowhere.
They are all one color like that field.

A nursing baby does not know the taste of roasted meat.
To a spirit the foodless scent is food.

To an Egyptian, the Nile looks bloody.
To an Israelite, clear.
What is a highway to one is disaster to the other.

THE NIGHT AIR

A man on his deathbed left instructions
for dividing up his goods among his three sons.
He had devoted his entire spirit to those sons.
They stood like cypress trees around him,
quiet and strong.
                    He told the town judge,
"Whichever of my sons is *laziest*,
give him *all* the inheritance."

Then he died, and the judge turned to the three,
"Each of you must give some account of your laziness,
so I can understand just *how* you are lazy."

Mystics are experts in laziness. They rely on it,
because they continuously see God working all around them.
The harvest keeps coming in, yet they
never even did the plowing!

"Come on. Say something about the ways you are lazy."

Every spoken word is a covering for the inner self.
A little curtain-flick no wider than a slice
of roast meat can reveal hundreds of exploding suns.
Even if what is being said is trivial and wrong,
the listener hears the source. One breeze comes

from across a garden. Another from across the ash-heap.
Think how different the voices of the fox
and the lion, and what they tell you!

Hearing someone is lifting the lid off the cooking pot.
You learn what's for supper. Though some people
can know just by the smell, a sweet stew
from a sour soup cooked with vinegar.

A man taps a clay pot before he buys it
to know by the sound if it has a crack.

The eldest of the three brothers told the judge,
"I can know a man by his voice,
                                    and if he won't speak,
I wait three days, and then I know him intuitively."

The second brother, "I know him when he speaks,
and if he won't talk, I strike up a conversation."

"But what if he knows that trick?" asked the judge.

Which reminds me of the mother who tells her child,
"When you're walking through the graveyard at night
and you see a boogeyman, run *at* it,
and it will go away."

"But what," replies the child, "if the boogeyman's
mother has told it to do the same thing?
Boogeymen have mothers too."

The second brother had no answer.

The judge then asked the youngest brother,
"What if a man cannot be made to say anything?
How do you learn his hidden nature?"

"I sit in front of him in silence,
and set up a ladder made of patience,
and if in his presence a language from beyond joy
and beyond grief begins to pour from *my* chest,
I know that his soul is as deep and bright
as the star Canopus rising over Yemen.

And so when I start speaking a powerful right arm
of words sweeping down, I know *him* from what I say,
and how I say it, because there's a window open
between us, mixing the night air of our beings."

The youngest was, obviously,
the laziest. He won.

ONLY BREATH

Not Christian or Jew or Muslim, not Hindu,
Buddhist, sufi, or zen. Not any religion

or cultural system. I am not from the East
or the West, not out of the ocean or up

from the ground, not natural or ethereal, not
composed of elements at all. I do not exist,

am not an entity in this world or the next,
did not descend from Adam and Eve or any

origin story. My place is placeless, a trace
of the traceless. Neither body or soul.

I belong to the beloved, have seen the two
worlds as one and that one call to and know,

first, last, outer, inner, only that
breath breathing human being.

There is a way between voice and presence
where information flows.

In disciplined silence it opens.
With wandering talk it closes.

4 ～ Spring Giddiness:

Stand in the Wake of This Chattering and Grow Airy

ON SPRING GIDDINESS

Springtime—when ecstasy seems the natural way to be and any other out of tune with the season of soul growth. Song, airy silence, a lively conversation between plants. No urgency about what gets said or not said. We feel part of some hilarious nub pulling up through the surface into light or lying back in a wagon going who knows where. The weather of Spring in Persia and Turkey and in the southeastern United States is all one long extravagant absorption with ground and sky, the fragrances and what unfolds from within. In lucky places such as these, Spring is not so much a metaphor for a state of attunement as it is that attunement. Or say it this way: for a mystic, the inner world is a weather that contains the universe and uses it as symbolic language.

SPRING

Again, the violet bows to the lily.
Again, the rose is tearing off her gown!

The green ones have come from the other world,
tipsy like the breeze up to some new foolishness.

Again, near the top of the mountain
the anemone's sweet features appear.

The hyacinth speaks formally to the jasmine,
"Peace be with you." "And peace to you, lad!
Come walk with me in this meadow."

Again, there are sufis everywhere!

The bud is shy, but the wind removes
her veil suddenly, "My friend!"

The Friend is here like water in the stream,
like a lotus on the water.

The narcissus winks at the wisteria,
"Whenever you say."

And the clove to the willow, "You are the one
I hope for." The willow replies, "Consider
these chambers of mine yours. Welcome!"

The apple, "Orange, why the frown?"
"So that those who mean harm
will not see my beauty."

The ringdove comes asking, "Where,
where is the Friend?"

With one note the nightingale
indicates the rose.

Again, the *season* of Spring has come
and a spring-source rises under everything,
a moon sliding from the shadows.

Many things must be left unsaid, because it's late,
but whatever conversation we haven't had
tonight, we'll have tomorrow.

WHERE EVERYTHING IS MUSIC

Don't worry about saving these songs!
And if one of our instruments breaks,
it doesn't matter.

We have fallen into the place
where everything is music.

The strumming and the flute notes
rise into the atmosphere,
and even if the whole world's harp
should burn up, there will still be
hidden instruments playing.

So the candle flickers and goes out.
We have a piece of flint, and a spark.

This singing art is sea foam.
The graceful movements come from a pearl
somewhere on the ocean floor.

Poems reach up like spindrift and the edge
of driftwood along the beach, wanting!

They derive
from a slow and powerful root
that we can't see.

Stop the words now.
Open the window in the center of your chest,
and let the spirits fly in and out.

A GREAT WAGON

When I see your face, the stones start spinning!
You appear; all studying wanders.
I lose my place.

Water turns pearly.
Fire dies down and doesn't destroy.

In your presence I don't want what I thought
I wanted, those three little hanging lamps.

Inside your face the ancient manuscripts
seem like rusty mirrors.

You breathe; new shapes appear,
and the music of a desire as widespread
as Spring begins to move
like a great wagon.
                    Drive slowly.
Some of us walking alongside
are lame!

꙳

Today, like every other day, we wake up empty
and frightened. Don't open the door to the study
and begin reading. Take down a musical instrument.

Let the beauty we love be what we do.
There are hundreds of ways to kneel and kiss the ground.

꙳

Out beyond ideas of wrongdoing and rightdoing,
there is a field. I'll meet you there.

When the soul lies down in that grass,
the world is too full to talk about.
Ideas, language, even the phrase *each other*
doesn't make any sense.

꙳

The breeze at dawn has secrets to tell you.
                    Don't go back to sleep.
You must ask for what you really want.
                    Don't go back to sleep.
People are going back and forth across the doorsill
                    where the two worlds touch.
The door is round and open.
                    Don't go back to sleep.

꙳

I would love to kiss you.
The price of kissing is your life.

Now my loving is running toward my life shouting,
What a bargain, let's buy it.

❧

Daylight, full of small dancing particles
and the one great turning, our souls
are dancing with you, without feet, they dance.
Can you see them when I whisper in your ear?

❧

They try to say what you are, spiritual or sexual?
They wonder about Solomon and all his wives.

In the body of the world, they say, there is a soul
and you are that.

But we have ways within each other
that will never be said by anyone.

❧

Come to the orchard in Spring.
There is light and wine, and sweethearts
        in the pomegranate flowers.

If you do not come, these do not matter.
If you do come, these do not matter.

SPRING IS CHRIST

Everyone has eaten and fallen asleep. The house is empty.
We walk out to the garden to let the apple meet the peach,
to carry messages between rose and jasmine.

Spring is Christ,
raising martyred plants from their shrouds.

Their mouths open in gratitude, wanting to be kissed.
The glow of the rose and the tulip means a lamp
is inside. A leaf trembles. I tremble
in the wind-beauty like silk from Turkestan.
The censer fans into flame.

This wind is the Holy Spirit.
The trees are Mary.
Watch how husband and wife play subtle games with their hands.
Cloudy pearls from Aden are thrown across the lovers,
as is the marriage custom.

The scent of Joseph's shirt comes to Jacob.
A red carnelian of Yemeni laughter is heard
by Muhammad in Mecca.

We talk about this and that. There's no rest
except on these branching moments.

SHREDS OF STEAM

Light again, and the one who brings light!
Change the way you live!

From the ocean vat, wine fire in each cup!
Two or three of the long dead wake up.
Two or three drunks become lion hunters.

Sunlight washes a dark face.
The flower of what's true opens in the face.
Meadowgrass and garden ground grow damp again.
A strong light like fingers massages our heads.
No dividing these fingers from those.

Draw back the lock bolt.
One level flows into another.
Heat seeps into everything.
The passionate pots boil.
Clothing tears into the air.
Poets fume shreds of steam,
never so happy as out in the light!

THE STEAMBATH

Steam fills the bath, and frozen figures on the wall
open their eyes, wet and round, Narcissus eyes
that see enormous distances, and new ears
that love the details of any story. The figures dance
like friends diving and coming up and diving again.

Steam spills into the courtyard. It's the noise
of resurrection! They move from one corner
laughing across to the opposite corner. No one notices
how steam opens the rose of each mind,
fills every beggar's cup solid with coins.
Hold out a basket. It fills up so well
that emptiness becomes what you want.

The judge and the accused forget the sentencing.
Someone stands up to speak, and the wood of the table
becomes holy. The tavern in that second is actually *made*
of wine. The dead drink it in.

> Then the steam evaporates.
Figures sink back into the wall, eyes blank,
ears just lines.

> Now it's happening again, outside.
The garden fills with bird and leaf sounds.

We stand in the wake of this chattering and grow airy.
How can anyone say what happens, even if each of us
dips a pen a hundred million times into ink?

THE GROUND CRIES OUT

I feel like the ground, astonished
at what the atmosphere has brought to it. What I know
is growing inside me. Rain makes
every molecule pregnant with a mystery.
We groan with women in labor.
The ground cries out, *I Am Truth* and *Glory Is Here*,
breaks open, and a camel is born out of it.
A branch falls from a tree, and there's a snake.

Muhammad said, *A faithful believer is a good camel,*
always looking to its master, who takes perfect care.
He brands the flank.
He sets out hay.
He binds the knees with reasonable rules,
and now he loosens all bindings and lets his camel dance,
tearing the bridle and ripping the blankets.

The field itself sprouts new forms,
while the camel dances over them, imaginary
plants no one has thought of,
but all these new seeds, no matter how they try,
do not reveal the other sun.
They hide it.
Still, the effort is joy,
one by one to keep uncovering
pearls in oyster shells.

UNFOLD YOUR OWN MYTH

Who gets up early to discover the moment light begins?
Who finds us here circling, bewildered, like atoms?
Who comes to a spring thirsty
and sees the moon reflected in it?
Who, like Jacob blind with grief and age,
smells the shirt of his lost son
and can see again?
Who lets a bucket down and brings up
a flowing prophet? Or like Moses goes for fire
and finds what burns inside the sunrise?

Jesus slips into a house to escape enemies,
and opens a door to the other world.
Solomon cuts open a fish, and there's a gold ring.
Omar storms in to kill the prophet
and leaves with blessings.
Chase a deer and end up everywhere!
An oyster opens his mouth to swallow one drop.
Now there's a pearl.

A vagrant wanders empty ruins.
Suddenly he's wealthy.

But don't be satisfied with stories, how things
have gone with others. Unfold
your own myth, without complicated explanation,
so everyone will understand the passage,
We have opened you.

Start walking toward Shams. Your legs will get heavy
and tired. Then comes a moment
of feeling the wings you've grown,
lifting.

NOT A DAY ON ANY CALENDAR

Spring, and everything outside is growing,
even the tall cypress tree.
We must not leave this place.
Around the lip of the cup we share, these words,

My Life Is Not Mine.

If someone were to play music, it would have to be very sweet.
We're drinking wine, but not through lips.
We're sleeping it off, but not in bed.
Rub the cup across your forehead.
This day is outside living and dying.

Give up wanting what other people have.
That way you're safe.
"Where, where can I be safe?" you ask.

This is not a day for asking questions,
not a day on any calendar.
This day is conscious of itself.
This day is a lover, bread, and gentleness,
more manifest than saying can say.

Thoughts take form with words,
but this daylight is beyond and before
thinking and imagining. Those two,

they are so thirsty, but this gives smoothness
to water. Their mouths are dry, and they are tired.

The rest of this poem is too blurry
for them to read.

FLUTES FOR DANCING

It's lucky to hear the flutes for dancing
coming down the road. The ground is glowing.
The table set in the yard.

We will drink all this wine tonight
because it's Spring. It is.
It's a growing sea. We're clouds
over the sea,
or flecks of matter
in the ocean when the ocean seems lit from within.
I know I'm drunk when I start this ocean talk.

Would you like to see the moon split
in half with one throw?

THE SHAPE OF MY TONGUE

This mirror inside me shows . . .
I can't say what, but I can't not know!

I run from body. I run from spirit.
I do not belong anywhere.

I'm not alive!
You smell the decay?

You talk about my craziness.
Listen rather to the honed-blade sanity I say.

This gourd head on top of a dervish robe,
do I look like someone you know?

This dipper gourd full of liquid,
upsidedown and not spilling a drop!

Or if it spills, it drops into God
and rounds into pearls.

I form a cloud over that ocean
and gather spillings.

When Shams is here,
I rain.

After a day or two, lilies sprout,
the shape of my tongue.

THE GRASSES

The same wind that uproots trees
makes the grasses shine.

The lordly wind loves the weakness
and the lowness of grasses.
Never brag of being strong.

The axe doesn't worry how thick the branches are.
It cuts them to pieces. But not the leaves.
It leaves the leaves alone.

A flame doesn't consider the size of the woodpile.
A butcher doesn't run from a flock of sheep.

What is form in the presence of reality?
Very feeble. Reality keeps the sky turned over
like a cup above us, revolving. Who turns
the sky wheel? The universal intelligence.

And the motion of the body comes
from the spirit like a waterwheel
that's held in a stream.

The inhaling-exhaling is from spirit,
now angry, now peaceful.

Wind destroys, and wind protects.

There is no reality but God,
says the completely surrendered sheikh,
who is an ocean for all beings.

The levels of creation are straws in that ocean.
The movement of the straws comes from an agitation
in the water. When the ocean wants the straws calm,
it sends them close to shore. When it wants them
back in the deep surge, it does with them
as the wind does with the grasses.

                                    This never ends.

THE SHEIKH WHO PLAYED WITH CHILDREN

A certain young man was asking around,
"I need to find a wise person. I have a problem."

A bystander said, "There's no one with intelligence
in our town except that man over there
playing with the children,

                         the one riding the stick-horse.

He has keen, fiery insight and vast dignity
like the night sky, but he conceals it
in the madness of child's play."

The young seeker approached the children, "Dear father,
you who have become as a child, tell me a secret."

"Go away. This is not a day
for secrets."

                  "But please! Ride your horse this way,
just for a minute."

                  The sheikh play-galloped over.
"Speak quickly. I can't hold this one still for long.
Whoops. Don't let him kick you.

                              This is a wild one!"

The young man felt he couldn't ask his serious question
in the crazy atmosphere, so he joked,
                              "I need to get married.
Is there someone suitable on this street?"

"There are three kinds of women in the world.
Two are griefs, and one is a treasure to the soul.
The first, when you marry her, is all yours.
The second is half-yours, and the third
is not yours at all.
                    Now get out of here,
before this horse kicks you in the head! Easy now!"

The sheikh rode off among the children.
The young man shouted, "Tell me more about the kinds of
    women!"

The sheikh, on his cane horsie, came closer,
"The virgin of your first love is all yours.
She will make you feel happy and free. A childless widow
is the second. She will be half-yours. The third,
who is nothing to you, is a married woman with a child.
By her first husband she had a child, and all her love
goes into that child. She will have no connection with you.
Now watch out.
              Back away.
                        I'm going to turn this rascal around!"

He gave a loud whoop and rode back,
calling the children around him.

"One more question, Master!"
                          The sheikh circled,
"What is it? Quickly! That rider over there needs me.
I think I'm in love."
                    "What is this playing that you do?
Why do you hide your intelligence so?"
                                    "The people here
want to put me in charge. They want me to be
judge, magistrate, and interpreter of all the texts.

The knowing I have doesn't want that. It wants to enjoy itself.
I am a plantation of sugarcane, and at the same time
I'm eating the sweetness."
                                    Knowledge that is acquired
is not like this. Those who have it worry if
audiences like it or not.
                              It's a bait for popularity.

Disputational knowing wants customers.
It has no soul.
                    Robust and energetic
before a responsive crowd, it slumps when no one is there.
The only real customer is God.
                                    Chew quietly
your sweet sugarcane God-Love, and stay
playfully childish.
                        Your face
will turn rosy with illumination
like the redbud flowers.

᠊ᢣ

Let the lover be disgraceful, crazy,
absentminded. Someone sober
will worry about things going badly.
Let the lover be.

᠊ᢣ

All day and night, music,
a quiet, bright
reedsong. If it
fades, we fade.

5 ⟶ *Feeling Separation:*
Don't Come Near Me

We know separation so well because we've tasted the union. The reed flute makes music because it has already experienced changing mud and rain and light into sugarcane. Longing becomes more poignant if in the distance you can't tell whether your friend is going away or coming back. The pushing away pulls you in. 4/18/98

SOMETIMES I FORGET COMPLETELY

Sometimes I forget completely
what companionship is.
Unconscious and insane, I spill sad
energy everywhere. My story
gets told in various ways: a romance,
a dirty joke, a war, a vacancy.

Divide up my forgetfulness to any number,
it will go around.
These dark suggestions that I follow,
are they part of some plan?
Friends, be careful. Don't come near me
out of curiosity, or sympathy.

A MAN AND A WOMAN ARGUING

One night in the desert
a poor Bedouin woman has this to say
to her husband,

"Everyone is happy
and prosperous, except us! We have no bread.
We have no spices. We have no water jug.
We barely have any clothes. No blankets

for the night. We fantasize that the full moon
is a cake. We reach for it! We're an embarrassment
even to the beggars. Everyone avoids us.

Arab men are supposed to be generous warriors,
but look at you, stumbling around! If some guest
were to come to us, we'd steal his rags
when he fell asleep. Who is your guide
that leads you to this? We can't even get
a handful of lentils! Ten years' worth
of nothing, that's what we are!"

                                    She went on and on.
"If God is abundant, we must be following
an imposter. Who's leading us? Some fake,
that always says, *Tomorrow, illumination
will bring you treasure, tomorrow.*

As everyone knows, that never comes.
Though I guess, it happens very rarely, sometimes,
that a disciple following an imposter can somehow
surpass the pretender. But still I want to know
what this deprivation says about us."

The husband replied, finally,

                                    "How long will you complain
about money and our prospects for money? The torrent
of our life has mostly gone by. Don't worry about
transient things. Think how the animals live.

The dove on the branch giving thanks.
The glorious singing of the nightingale.
The gnat. The elephant. Every living thing
trusts in God for its nourishment.

These pains that you feel are messengers.
Listen to them. Turn them to sweetness. The night

is almost over. You were young once, and content.
Now you think about money all the time.

You used to *be* that money. You were a healthy vine.
Now you're a rotten fruit. You ought to be growing
sweeter and sweeter, but you've gone bad.
As my wife, you should be equal to me.
Like a pair of boots, if one is too tight,
the pair is of no use.

Like two folding doors, we can't be mismatched.
A lion does not mate with a wolf."

So this man who was happily poor
scolded his wife until daybreak,
when she responded,
                    "Don't talk to me
about your high station! Look how you act!
Spiritual arrogance is the ugliest of all things.
It's like a day that's cold and snowy,
and your clothes are wet too!

It's too much to bear!
And don't call me your mate, you fraud!
You scramble after scraps of bone
with the dogs.

You're not as satisfied as you pretend!
You're the snake and the snake charmer
at the same time, but you don't know it.
You're charming a snake for money,
and the snake is charming you.

You talk about God a lot, and you make me feel guilty
by using that word. You better watch out!
That word will poison you, if you use it
to have power over me."

So the rough volume of her talking
fell on the husband, and he fought back,
                                        "Woman,

49

this poverty is my deepest joy.
This bare way of life is honest and beautiful.
We can hide nothing when we're like this.
You say I'm really arrogant and greedy,
and you say I'm a snake charmer and a snake,
but those nicknames are for you.

In your anger and your wantings
you see those qualities in me.
I want nothing from this world.

You're like a child that has turned round and round,
and now you think the house is turning.

It's your eyes that see wrong. Be patient,
and you'll see the blessings and the lord's light
in how we live."
                    This argument continued
throughout the day, and even longer.

⟡

A night full of talking that hurts,
my worst held-back secrets. Everything
has to do with loving and not loving.
This night will pass.
Then we have work to do.

⟡

AN EMPTY GARLIC

You miss the garden,
because you want a small fig from a random tree.
You don't meet the beautiful woman.
You're joking with an old crone.
It makes me want to cry how she detains you,
stinking mouthed, with a hundred talons,
putting her head over the roof edge to call down,

tasteless fig, fold over fold, empty
as dry-rotten garlic.

She has you tight by the belt,
even though there's no flower and no milk
inside her body.
Death will open your eyes
to what her face is: leather spine
of a black lizard. No more advice.

Let yourself be silently drawn
by the stronger pull of what you really love.

THE DIVER'S CLOTHES LYING EMPTY

You're sitting here with us, but you're also out walking
in a field at dawn. You are yourself
the animal we hunt when you come with us on the hunt.
You're in your body like a plant is solid in the ground,
yet you're wind. You're the diver's clothes
lying empty on the beach. You're the fish.

In the ocean are many bright strands
and many dark strands like veins that are seen
when a wing is lifted up.
Your hidden self is blood in those, those veins
that are lute strings that make ocean music,
not the sad edge of surf, but the sound of no shore.

RED SHIRT

Has anyone seen the boy who used to come here?
Round-faced troublemaker, quick to find a joke, slow
to be serious. Red shirt,
perfect coordination, sly,
strong muscles, with things always in his pocket: reed flute,
ivory pick, polished and ready for his talent.
You know that one.

Have you heard stories about him?
Pharaoh and the whole Egyptian world
collapsed for such a Joseph.
I'd gladly spend years getting word
of him, even third or fourth-hand.

MY WORST HABIT

My worst habit is I get so tired of winter
I become a torture to those I'm with.

If you're not here, nothing grows.
I lack clarity. My words
tangle and knot up.

How to cure bad water? Send it back to the river.
How to cure bad habits? Send me back to you.

When water gets caught in habitual whirlpools,
dig a way out through the bottom
to the ocean. There is a secret medicine
given only to those who hurt so hard
they can't hope.

The hopers would feel slighted if they knew.

Look as long as you can at the friend you love,
no matter whether that friend is moving away from you
or coming back toward you.

ॐ

Don't let your throat tighten
with fear. Take sips of breath
all day and night, before death
closes your mouth.

ॐ

DISSOLVER OF SUGAR

Dissolver of sugar, dissolve me,
if this is the time.
Do it gently with a touch of a hand, or a look.
Every morning I wait at dawn. That's when
it's happened before. Or do it suddenly
like an execution. How else
can I get ready for death?

You breathe without a body like a spark.
You grieve, and I begin to feel lighter.
You keep me away with your arm,
but the keeping away is pulling me in.

Pale sunlight,
pale the wall.

Love moves away.
The light changes.

I need more grace
than I thought.

6 ↗ Controlling the Desire-Body: How Did You Kill Your Rooster, Husam?

ON THE DESIRE-BODY

Sufis call the wantings nafs. *From the urgent way lovers want each other to the sannyasin's search for truth, all moving is from the mover. Every pull draws us to the ocean. Rumi says it's important to live the wantings as they come and not get stuck somewhere, stagnant. He was asked once what to do about a young man caught doing some indecent act. The story doesn't mention what exactly—masturbation, peeping-tomming, whatever wild wantings young men think to do. Rumi told them not to worry about it. "It just means he's growing his feathers. The dangerous case is a kid who doesn't do indecent acts, who then leaves the nest without feathers. One flap and the cat has him." Be careful, Rumi suggests, about shaming sexual behavior in an adolescent or anyone who hasn't yet had his or her fill of erotic trancing. Often, the closest we come to surrender is orgasm. In Rumi's symbology the rooster is a symbol for that energy.*

So how did Husam kill his rooster? By dissolving into the play. The nafs *are energies that keep us moving, stopping nowhere. Union with the divine continually unfolds. Next to the glowing drive-in movie, the junkyard's rusted stacks of old desire-bodies. Let the beauty we love keep turning into action, transmuting to another, another. What have I ever lost by dying? Rumi asks, exchanging one set of* nafs *for the next. Chopped rooster energy becomes another dining room story. Particles of praise shine in the sunlight. Anything you grab hold of on the bank breaks with the river's pressure. When you do things from your soul, the river itself moves through you. Freshness and a deep joy are signs of the current.*

Someone offhand to the Caliph of Egypt,
"The King of Mosul
has a concubine like no other,
more beautiful than I can describe.
She looks like *this*."
He draws her likeness on paper.

The Caliph drops his cup.
Immediately he sends his captain to Mosul
with an army of thousands. The siege goes on for a week,
with many casualties, the walls and the towers unsteady,
as soft as wax. The King of Mosul sends an envoy.
"Why this killing? If you want the city,
I will leave and you can have it!
If you want more wealth, that's even easier."

The captain takes out the piece of paper
with the girl's picture on it. This.
The strong King of Mosul is quick to reply.
"Lead her out. The idol belongs with the idolater."

When the captain sees her, he falls in love
like the Caliph. Don't laugh at this.
This loving is also part of infinite love,
without which the world does not evolve.
Objects move from inorganic to vegetation
to selves endowed with spirit through the urgency
of every love that wants to come to perfection.

This captain thinks the soil looks fertile,
so he sows his seed. Sleeping, he sees the girl
in a dream. He makes love to her image,
and his semen spurts out.

After a while he begins to wake.
Slowly he senses the girl is not there.
"I have given my seed into nothing.
I shall put this tricky woman to a test."

A leader who is not captain of his body is not one
to be honored, with his semen spilled so in the sand.
Now he loses all control. He doesn't care
about the Caliph, or about dying.
"I am in love," he says.

Do not act in such heat.
Take counsel with a master.
But the captain couldn't.

His infatuation is a blackwater wave carrying him away.
Something that doesn't exist makes a phantom
appear in the darkness of a well,
and the phantom itself becomes strong enough
to throw actual lions into the hole.

More advice: it is dangerous to let other men
have intimate connections with the women in your care.
Cotton and fire sparks, those are, together.
Difficult, almost impossible, to quench.

The captain does not return straight to the Caliph,
but instead camps in a secluded meadow.
Blazing, he can't tell ground from sky.
His reason is lost in a drumming sound,
worthless radish and son of a radish.
The Caliph himself a gnat, nothing.

But just as this cultivator tears off the woman's pants
and lies down between her legs, his penis moving
straight to the mark, there's a great tumult
and a rising cry of soldiers outside the tent.
He leaps up with his bare bottom shining
and runs out, scimitar in hand.

A black lion from a nearby swamp
has gotten in among the horses. Chaos.
The lion jumping twenty feet in the air,
tents billowing like an ocean.

The captain quickly approaches the lion,
splits his head with one blow,
and now he's running back to the woman's tent.

When he stretches out her beauty again,
his penis goes even more erect.

The engagement, the coming together, is as with the lion.
His penis stays erect all through it,
and it does not scatter semen feebly.
The beautiful one is amazed at his virility.
Immediately, with great energy she joins with his energy,
and their two spirits go out from them as one.

Whenever two are linked this way, there comes another
from the unseen world. It may be through birth,
if nothing prevents conception,
but a third does come, when two unite in love,
or in hate. The intense qualities born
of such joining appear in the spiritual world.

You will recognize them when you go there.
Your associations bear progeny.
Be careful, therefore. Wait, and be conscious,
before you go to meet anyone.
Remember there are children to consider!

Children you must live with and tend to,
born of your emotions with another, entities
with a form, and speech, and a place to live.
They are crying to you even now.
You have forgotten us. Come back.
Be aware of this. A man and a woman together
always have a spiritual result.

The captain was not so aware. He fell,
and stuck like a gnat in a pot of buttermilk,
totally absorbed in his love affair. Then,
just as suddenly, he's uninterested. He tells
the woman, "Don't say a word of this to the Caliph."

He takes her there, and the Caliph is smitten.
She's a hundred times more beautiful than he's imagined.

A certain man asks an eloquent teacher,
"What is true and what false?" "This is false:
a bat hides from the sun, not from the idea of the sun.

It's the idea that puts fear in the bat and leads it
deeper into the cave. You have an idea
of an enemy that attaches you to certain companions.

Moses, the inner light of revelation,
lit up the top of Sinai, but the mountain
could not hold that light.

Don't deceive yourself that way!
Having the idea is not living
the reality, of anything.

There's no courage in the idea of battle.
The bathhouse wall is covered with pictures
and much talk of heroism. Try to make an idea move
from ear to eye. Then your woolly ears
become as subtle as fibers of light.

Your whole body becomes a mirror,
all eye and spiritual breathing.
Let your ear lead you to your lover."

So the Caliph is mightily in love with this girl.
His kingdom vanishes like lightning.
If your loving is numb, know this: when what you own
can vanish, it's only a dream, a vanity, breath
through a mustache. It would have killed you.

There are those that say, "Nothing lasts."
They're wrong. Every moment they say,
"If there were some other reality,
I would have seen it. I would know about it."

Because a child doesn't understand a chain of reasoning,
should adults give up being rational?
If reasonable people don't feel the presence of love
within the universe, that doesn't mean it's not there.

Joseph's brothers did not see Joseph's beauty,
but Jacob never lost sight of it. Moses at first
saw only a wooden staff, but to his other seeing
it was a viper and a cause of panic.

Eyesight is in conflict with inner knowing.
Moses' hand is a hand and a source of light.

These matters are as real as the infinite is real,
but they seem religious fantasies to some,
to those who believe only in the reality
of the sexual organs and the digestive tract.

Don't mention the Friend to those.
To others, sex and hunger are fading images,
and the Friend is more constantly, solidly here.
Let the former go to their church, and we'll go to ours.
Don't talk long to skeptics or to those
who claim to be atheists.

So the Caliph has the idea
of entering the beautiful woman,
and he comes to her to do his wanting.

Memory raises his penis, straining it in thought
toward the pushing down and the lifting up
which make that member grow large with delight.

But as he actually lies down with the woman,
there comes to him a decree from God
to stop these voluptuous doings. A very tiny sound,
like a mouse might make. The penis droops,
and desire slips away.

He thinks that whispering sound is a snake
rising off the straw mat. The girl sees his drooping
and sails into fits of laughing at the marvelous thing.
She remembers the captain killing the lion
with his penis standing straight up.

Long and loud her laughter.
Anything she thinks of only increases it,
like the laughter of those who eat hashish.
Everything is funny.

Every emotion has a source and a key that opens it.
The Caliph is furious. He draws his sword.
"What's so amusing? Tell me everything you're thinking.

Don't hold anything back. At this moment
I'm clairvoyant. If you lie, I'll behead you.
If you tell the truth, I'll give you your freedom."

He stacks seven Qur'ans on top of each other
and swears to do as he says.
When she finally gets hold of herself,
the girl tells all, in great detail. Of the camp
in the meadow, the killing of the lion,
the captain's return to the tent with his penis
still hard as the horn of a rhino.

And the contrast with the Caliph's own member
sinking down because of one mouse-whisper.
Hidden things always come to light.
Do not sow bad seed. Be sure, they'll come up.
Rain and the sun's heat make them rise into the air.
Spring comes after the fall of the leaves,
which is proof enough of the fact of resurrection.
Secrets come out in Spring, out from earth-lips into leaf.
Worries become wine-headaches.
But where did the wine come from? Think.

A branch of blossoms does not look like seed.
A man does not resemble semen. Jesus came
from Gabriel's breath, but he is not in that form.
The grape doesn't look like the vine.
Loving actions are the seed of something
completely different, a living-place.
No origin is like where it leads to.
We can't know where our pain is from.
We don't know all that we've done.
Perhaps it's best that we don't.
Nevertheless we suffer for it.

The Caliph comes back to his clarity. "In the pride
of my power I took this woman from another,
so of course, someone came to knock on my door.
Whoever commits adultery is a pimp
for his own wife.

If you cause injury to someone, you draw
that same injury toward yourself. My treachery
made my friend a traitor to me. This repetition
must stop somewhere. Here, in an act of mercy.

I'll send you back to the captain,
saying another of my wives is jealous,
and since the captain was brave enough
to bring you back from Mosul,
he shall have you in marriage."

This is the virility of a prophet.
The Caliph was sexually impotent,
but his manliness was most powerful.

The kernel of true manhood is the ability
to abandon sensual indulgences. The intensity
of the captain's libido is less than a husk
compared to the Caliph's nobility in ending
the cycle of sowing lust and reaping
secrecy and vengefulness.

TATTOOING IN QAZWIN

In Qazwin, they have a custom of tattooing themselves
for good luck, with a blue ink, on the back
of the hand, the shoulder, wherever.

A certain man there goes to his barber
and asks to be given a powerful, heroic, blue lion
on his shoulder blade. "And do it with flair!
I've got Leo ascending. I want plenty of blue!"

But as soon as the needle starts pricking,
he howls,
              "What are you doing?"
                              "The lion."
"Which limb did you start with?"
                              "I began with the tail."
"Well, leave out the tail. That lion's rump
is in a bad place for me. It cuts off my wind."

The barber continues, and immediately
the man yells out,
              "Oooooooo! Which part now?"
                                        "The ear."
"Doc, let's do a lion with no ears this time."
                              The barber
shakes his head, and once more the needle,
and once more the wailing,
                    "Where are you now?"
                                        "The belly."
"I like a lion without a belly."
                        The master lion-maker
stands for a long time with his fingers in his teeth.
Finally, he throws the needle down.
                          "No one has ever
been asked to do such a thing! To create a lion
without a tail or a head or a stomach.
God himself could not do it!"

Brother, stand the pain.
Escape the poison of your impulses.
The sky will bow to your beauty, if you do.
Learn to light the candle. Rise with the sun.
Turn away from the cave of your sleeping.
That way a thorn expands to a rose.
A particular glows with the universal.

What is it to praise?
Make yourself particles.

What is it to know something of God?
Burn inside that presence. Burn up.

Copper melts in the healing elixir.
So melt your self in the mixture
that sustains existence.

You tighten your two hands together,
determined not to give up saying "I" and "we."
This tightening blocks you.

No more wine for me!
I'm past delighting in the thick red
and the clear white.

I'm thirsty for my own blood
as it moves into a field of action.

Draw the keenest blade you have
and strike, until the head circles
about the body.

Make a mountain of skulls like that.
Split me apart.

Don't stop at the mouth!
Don't listen to anything I say.
I must enter the center of the fire.

Fire is my child
but I must be consumed
and become fire.

Why is there crackling and smoke?
Because the firewood and the flames
are still talking:
    "You are too dense. Go away!"
"You are too wavering. I have solid form."

In the blackness those two friends keep arguing.
Like a wanderer with no face.
Like the most powerful bird in existence
sitting on its perch, refusing to move.

What can I say to someone so curled up with wanting,
so constricted in his love?

Break your pitcher against a rock.
We don't need any longer
to haul pieces of the ocean around.

We must drown, away from heroism,
and descriptions of heroism.

Like a pure spirit lying down, pulling
its body over it, like a bride her husband
for a cover to keep her warm.

🙬

Someone who goes with half a loaf of bread
to a small place that fits like a nest around him,
someone who wants no more, who's not himself
longed for by anyone else,

He is a letter to everyone. You open it.
It says, *Live*.

🙬

The mystery does not get clearer by repeating the question,
nor is it bought with going to amazing places.

Until you've kept your eyes
and your wanting still for fifty years,
you don't begin to cross over from confusion.

MUHAMMAD AND THE HUGE EATER

Husam demands that we begin Book V.
Ziya-Haqq, the radiance of truth,

Husamuddin,
master to the pure masters,
if my human throat were not so narrow,
I would praise you as you should be praised,
in some language other than this word-language,
but a domestic fowl is not a falcon.
We must mix the varnish we have
and brush it on.

I'm not talking to materialists. When I mention Husam,
I speak only to those who know spiritual secrets.
Praise is simply drawing back the curtains
to let his qualities in.

The sun,

of course, remains apart
from what I say.

What the sayer of praise is really praising is
himself, by saying implicitly,
"My eyes are clear."

Likewise, someone who criticizes is criticizing
himself, saying implicitly, "I can't see very well
with my eyes so inflamed."

Don't ever feel sorry for someone
who wants to be the sun, that other sun,
the one that makes rotten things fresh.

And don't ever envy someone
who wants to be this world.

Husam is the sun I mean.
He can't be understood with the mind, or said,
but we'll stumble and stagger trying to.
Just because you can't drink all that falls
doesn't mean you give up taking sips
of rainwater. If the nut
of the mystery can't be held,
at least let me touch the shell.

Husam, refresh my words, your words.
My words are only a husk to your knowing,
an earth atmosphere to your enormous spaces.

What I say is meant only to point to that, to you,
so that whoever ever hears these words will not grieve
that they never had a chance to look.

Your presence draws me out from vanity
and imagination and opinion.

Awe is the salve
that will heal our eyes.

And keen, constant listening.
Stay out in the open like a date palm
lifting its arms. Don't bore mouse holes

in the ground, arguing inside some
doctrinal labyrinth.

That intellectual warp and woof keeps you wrapped
in blindness. And four other characteristics
keep you from loving. The Qur'an calls them
four birds. Say *Bismillah,* "In the name of God,"
and chop the heads off those mischief-birds.

The rooster of lust, the peacock of wanting
to be famous, the crow of ownership, and the duck
of urgency, kill them and revive them
in another form, changed and harmless.

There is a duck inside you.
Her bill is never still, searching through dry
and wet alike, like the robber in an empty house
cramming objects in his sack, pearls, chickpeas,
anything. Always thinking, "There's no time!
I won't get another chance!"

A True Person is more calm and deliberate.
He or she doesn't worry about interruptions.

But that duck is so afraid of missing out
that it's lost all generosity, and frighteningly expanded
its capacity to take in food.

A large group of unbelievers
once came to see Muhammad,
knowing he would feed them.

Muhammad told his friends,
"Divide these guests among you and tend to them.
Since you are all filled with me,
it will be as though I am the host."

Each friend of Muhammad chose a guest,
but there was one huge person left behind.
He sat in the entrance of the mosque
like thick dregs in a cup.

So Muhammad invited the man to his own household,
where the enormous son of a Ghuzz Turk ate everything,

the milk of seven goats and enough food
for eighteen people!

The others in the house were furious.
When the man went to bed, the maid slammed the door
behind him and chained it shut, out of meanness
and resentment. Around midnight, the man
felt several strong urges at once.

But the door! He works it,
puts a blade through the crack. Nothing.
The urgency increases. The room contracts.
He falls back into a confused sleep and dreams
of a desolate place, since he himself is
such a desolate place.

So, dreaming he's by himself,
he squeezes out a huge amount,
and another huge amount.

But he soon becomes conscious enough
to know that the covers he gathers around him
are full of shit. He shakes with spasms of the shame
that usually keeps men from doing such things.

He thinks, "My sleep is worse than my being awake.
The waking is just full of food.
My sleep is all *this*."

Now he's crying, bitterly embarrassed,
waiting for dawn and the noise of the door opening,
hoping that somehow he can get out
without anyone seeing him as he is.

I'll shorten it. The door opens. He's saved.
Muhammad comes at dawn. He opens the door
and becomes invisible so the man won't feel ashamed,
so he can escape and wash himself
and not have to face the door-opener.

Someone completely absorbed in Allah like Muhammad
can do this. Muhammad had seen all that went on

in the night, but he held back from letting the man out,
until all happened as it needed to happen.

Many actions which seem cruel
are from a deep friendship.
Many demolitions are actually renovations.

Later, a meddlesome servant
brought Muhammad the bedclothes.
"Look what your guest has done!"

Muhammad smiles, himself a mercy given to all beings,
"Bring me a bucket of water."

Everyone jumps up, "No! Let us do this.
We live to serve you, and this is the kind of hand-work
we can do. Yours is the inner heart-work."

"I know that, but this is an extraordinary occasion."

A voice inside him is saying, "There is great wisdom
in washing these bedclothes. Wash them."

Meanwhile, the man who soiled the covers and fled
is returning to Muhammad's house. He has left behind
an amulet that he always carried.

He enters and sees the hands of God
washing his incredibly dirty linen.

He forgets the amulet. A great love suddenly enters him.
He tears his shirt open. He strikes his head
against the wall and the door. Blood
pours from his nose.

People come from other parts of the house.
He's shrieking, "Stay away!"
He hits his head, "I have no understanding!"
He prostrates himself before Muhammad.

"You are the whole. I am a despicable, tiny,
meaningless piece. I can't look at you."
He's quiet and quivering with remorse.

Muhammad bends over and holds him and caresses him
and opens his inner knowing.

The cloud weeps, and then the garden sprouts.
The baby cries, and the mother's milk flows.
The nurse of creation has said, *Let them cry a lot.*

This rain-weeping and sun-burning twine together
to make us grow. Keep your intelligence white-hot
and your grief glistening, so your life will stay fresh.
Cry easily like a little child.

Let body needs dwindle and soul decisions increase.
Diminish what you give your physical self.
Your spiritual eye will begin to open.

When the body empties and stays empty,
God fills it with musk and mother-of-pearl.
That way a man gives his dung and gets purity.

Listen to the prophets, not to some adolescent boy.
The foundation and the walls of the spiritual life
are made of self-denials and disciplines.

Stay with friends who support you in these.
Talk with them about sacred texts,
and how you're doing, and how they're doing,
and keep your practices together.

FASTING

There's hidden sweetness in the stomach's emptiness.
We are lutes, no more, no less. If the soundbox
is stuffed full of anything, no music.
If the brain and the belly are burning clean
with fasting, every moment a new song comes out of the fire.
The fog clears, and new energy makes you
run up the steps in front of you.
Be emptier and cry like reed instruments cry.
Emptier, write secrets with the reed pen.
When you're full of food and drink, an ugly metal
statue sits where your spirit should. When you fast,

good habits gather like friends who want to help.
Fasting is Solomon's ring. Don't give it
to some illusion and lose your power,
but even if you have, if you've lost all will and control,
they come back when you fast, like soldiers appearing
out of the ground, pennants flying above them.
A table descends to your tents,
Jesus' table.
Expect to see it, when you fast, this table
spread with other food, better than the broth of cabbages.

BISMILLAH

It's a habit of yours to walk slowly.
You hold a grudge for years.
With such heaviness, how can you be modest?
With such attachments, do you expect to arrive anywhere?

Be wide as the air to learn a secret.
Right now you're equal portions clay
and water, thick mud.

Abraham learned how the sun and moon and the stars all set.
He said, *No longer will I try to assign partners for God.*

You are so weak. Give up to grace.
The ocean takes care of each wave
till it gets to shore.
You need more help than you know.
You're trying to live your life in open scaffolding.
Say Bismillah, *In the name of God,*
as the priest does with a knife when he offers an animal.

Bismillah your old self
to find your real name.

WEAN YOURSELF

Little by little, wean yourself.
This is the gist of what I have to say.

From an embryo, whose nourishment comes in the blood,
move to an infant drinking milk,
to a child on solid food,
to a searcher after wisdom,
to a hunter of more invisible game.

Think how it is to have a conversation with an embryo.
You might say, "The world outside is vast and intricate.
There are wheatfields and mountain passes,
and orchards in bloom.

At night there are millions of galaxies, and in sunlight
the beauty of friends dancing at a wedding."

You ask the embryo why he, or she, stays cooped up
in the dark with eyes closed.

                              Listen to the answer.

There is no "other world."
I only know what I've experienced.
You must be hallucinating.

AFTER THE MEDITATION

Now I see something in my listeners
that won't let me continue this way.

The ocean flows back in
and puts up a foam barrier,
and then withdraws.

After a while,
it will come in again.

This audience wants to hear more
about the visiting sufi and his friends
in meditation. But be discerning.

Don't think of this as a normal character
in an ordinary story.

The ecstatic meditation ended.
Dishes of food were brought out.

The sufi remembered his donkey
that had carried him all day.

He called to the servant there, "Please,
go to the stable and mix the barley generously
with the straw for the animal. Please."

"Don't worry yourself with such matters.
All things have been attended to."

"But I want to make sure that you wet the barley first.
He's an old donkey, and his teeth are shaky."
"Why are you telling me this?
I have given the appropriate orders."

"But did you remove the saddle gently,
and put salve on the sore he has?"

"I have served thousands of guests
with these difficulties, and all have gone away
satisfied. Here, you are treated as family.
Do not worry. Enjoy yourself."

"But did you warm his water
just a little, and then add only a bit of straw
to the barley?"

                    "Sir, I'm ashamed for you."

                                        "And please,
sweep the stall clean of stones and dung,
and scatter a little dry earth in it."

"For God's sake, sir,
leave my business to *me!*"

"And did you currycomb his back?
He loves that."

                    "Sir! I am *personally*
responsible for all these chores!"

The servant turned and left at a brisk pace . . .
to join his friends in the street.

The sufi then lay down to sleep
and had terrible dreams about his donkey,

how it was being torn to pieces by a wolf,
or falling helplessly into a ditch.

And his dreaming was right!
His donkey was being totally neglected, weak and gasping,
without food or water all the night long.
The servant had done nothing he said he would.

There are such vicious and empty flatterers
in your life. Do the careful,
donkey-tending work.

Don't trust that to anyone else.
There are hypocrites who will praise you,
but who do not care about the health
of your heart-donkey.
                    Be concentrated and leonine
in the hunt for what is your true nourishment.
Don't be distracted by blandishment-noises,
of any sort.

THE DOG IN THE DOORWAY

This is how it is when your animal energies,
the *nafs,* dominate your soul:

You have a piece of fine linen
that you're going to make into a coat
to give to a friend, but someone else uses it
to make a pair of pants. The linen
has no choice in the matter.
It must submit. Or, it's like
someone breaks into your house
and goes to the garden and plants thornbushes.
An ugly humiliation falls over the place.

Or, you've seen a nomad's dog
lying at the tent entrance, with his head
on the threshold and his eyes closed.

Children pull his tail and touch his face,
but he doesn't move. He loves the children's
attention and stays humble within it.

But if a stranger walks by, he'll spring up
ferociously. Now, what if that dog's owner
were not able to control it?

A poor dervish might appear: the dog storms out.
The dervish says, "I take refuge with God
when the dog of arrogance attacks,"
and the owner has to say, "So do I!
I'm helpless against this creature
even in my own house!

Just as you can't come close,
I can't go out!"

This is how animal energy becomes monstrous
and ruins your life's freshness and beauty.

Think of taking this dog out to hunt!
You'd be the quarry.

🦢

The light you give off
did not come from a pelvis.

Your features did not begin in semen.
Don't try to hide inside anger
radiance that cannot be hidden.

🦢

TENDING TWO SHOPS

Don't run around this world
looking for a hole to hide in.

There are wild beasts in *every* cave!
If you live with mice,
the cat claws will find you.

The only real rest comes
when you're alone with God.

Live in the nowhere that you came from,
even though you have an address here.

That's why you see things in two ways.
Sometimes you look at a person
and see a cynical snake.

Someone else sees a joyful lover,
and you're both right!

Everyone is half and half,
like the black and white ox.

Joseph looked ugly to his brothers,
and most handsome to his father.

You have eyes that see from that nowhere,
and eyes that judge distances,
how high and how low.

You own two shops,
and you run back and forth.

Try to close the one that's a fearful trap,
getting always smaller. Checkmate,
this way. Checkmate that.

Keep open the shop
where you're not selling fishhooks anymore.
You are the free-swimming fish.

❦

Think that you're gliding out from the face of a cliff
like an eagle. Think you're walking
like a tiger walks by himself in the forest.
You're most handsome when you're after food.

Spend less time with nightingales and peacocks.
One is just a voice, the other just a color.

7 ❧ Sohbet:

Meetings on the Riverbank

ON *SOHBET*

Sohbet *has no English equivalent. It means something like "mystical conversation on mystical subjects." The voices in Rumi's poetry come from many points on the inner-outer spectrum. The outer conversations are contained within quotation marks, and the inner ones are continuous and permeate the entire fabric of his poetry. On the most ordinary level, we all sometimes hear ourselves speaking from, say, some habitual pattern of meanness or acceptable optimism; then at other times we surprise ourselves by coming out with wisdom beyond our usual. There's a modulation between realities. This is similar to what happens with the fluid pronoun in Rumi's poetry. The* you *and* I *are sometimes the lover talking to the beloved, the personal self and a without-form presence within and beyond the senses. Yet sometimes that presence, amazingly, speaks to Rumi through the poetry; voices slide back and forth within the same short poem! Often the poem serves as a slippery doorsill place between the two, "partly in my self and partly outside," the voices coming from a between-place. This expanding and contracting of identity is one of the exciting aspects of Rumi's art. Everything is conversation.*

> Human beings are discourse. That flowing moves through you
> whether you say anything or not. Everything that happens is filled
> with pleasure and warmth because of the delight of the discourse
> that's always going on.
>
> DISCOURSE 53

Rumi's poetry mirrors back to us this ocean of woven speech too intricate and dynamic for any grammarian to untangle.

In the middle of the night,
I cried out,
          "Who lives in this love
I have?"
          You said, "I do, but I'm not here
alone. Why are these other images
with me?"
          I said, "They are reflections of you,
just as the beautiful inhabitants of Chigil
in Turkestan resemble each other."

You said, "But who is this other *living*
being?"
          "That is my wounded soul."
Then I brought that soul
to you as a prisoner.
                    "This one is dangerous,"
I said. "Don't let him off easy."

You winked and gave me one end
of a delicate thread.
                    "Pull it tight,
but don't break it."
                    I reached my hand
to touch you. You struck it down.

"Why are you so harsh with me?"

"For good reason. But certainly not
to keep you away! Whoever enters this place
saying *Here I am* must be slapped.

This is not a pen for sheep.

There are no separating distances here.
This is love's sanctuary.

Saladin is how the soul looks. Rub your eyes,
and look again with love at love."

You said, "Who's at the door?"
    I said, "Your slave."

You said, "What do you want?"
    "To see you and bow."

"How long will you wait?"
    "Until you call."

"How long will you cook?"
    "Till the Resurrection."

We talked through the door. I claimed
a great love and that I had given up
what the world gives to be in that love.

You said, "Such claims require a witness."
    I said, "This longing, these tears."

You said, "Discredited witnesses."
    I said, "Surely not!"

You said, "Who did you come with?"
    "The majestic imagination you gave me."

"*Why* did you come?"
    "The musk of your wine was in the air."

"What is your intention?"
    "Friendship."

"What do you want from me?"
    "Grace."

Then you asked, "Where have you been
most comfortable?"
    "In the palace."

"What did you see there?"
    "Amazing things."

"Then why is it so desolate?"
    "Because all that can be taken away in a second."

"Who can do that?"
        "This clear discernment."

"Where can you live safely then?"
        "In surrender."

"What is this giving up?"
        "A peace that saves us."

"Is there no threat of disaster?"
        "Only what comes in your street,
        inside your love."

"How do you walk there?"
        "In perfection."

Now silence. If I told more of this conversation,
those listening would leave themselves.

There would be no door,
no roof or window either!

A MOUSE AND A FROG

A mouse and a frog meet every morning on the riverbank.
They sit in a nook of the ground and talk.

Each morning, the second they see each other,
they open easily, telling stories and dreams and secrets,
empty of any fear or suspicious holding back.

To watch and listen to those two
is to understand how, as it's written,
sometimes when two beings come together,
Christ becomes visible.

The mouse starts laughing out a story he hasn't thought of
in five years, and the telling might take five years!
There's no blocking the speechflow-river-running-
all-carrying momentum that true intimacy is.

Bitterness doesn't have a chance
with those two.

The God-messenger, Khidr, touches a roasted fish.
It leaps off the grill back into the water.

Friend sits by Friend, and the tablets appear.
They read the mysteries
off each other's foreheads.

But one day the mouse complains, "There are times
when I want *sohbet,* and you're out in the water,
jumping around where you can't hear me.

We meet at this appointed time,
but the text says, *Lovers pray constantly.*

Once a day, once a week, five times an hour,
is not enough. Fish like we are
need the ocean around us!"

Do camel bells say, *Let's meet back here Thursday night?*
Ridiculous. They jingle
together continuously,
talking while the camel walks.

Do you pay regular visits to *yourself?*
Don't argue or answer rationally.

Let us die,
            and dying, reply.

THE LONG STRING

The mouse asks the beloved frog,

                              "Do you know
what you are to me? During the day,
you're my energy for working. At night,
you're my deepest sleep.

                    But could we be together
outside of time as well as inside?

Physically, we meet only at breakfast.
Your absence during the rest of the day

enters all my cravings!
                                I drink
five hundred times too much.
                                                I eat
like a bulimic trying to die.
                                                Help me!

I know I'm not worth it,
but your generosity is so vast!

Let your sunlight shine on this piece of dung,
and dry it out, so I can be used for fuel
to warm and light up a bathhouse.

Look on the terrible and stupid things I've done,
and cause herbs and eglantine to grow out of them.

The sun does this with the ground.
Think what glories God can make
from the fertilizer of sinning!

The mouse continues to beg, "My friend,
I know I'm ugly to you.
                                        I'm ugly to me!
I'm perfectly ugly!
                        But look, you'll be sad
when I die, won't you? You'll sit by my grave
and weep a little?
                        All I'm asking is,
be with me that little bit of time
while I'm still alive!
Now. I want you *NOW!*"

A certain rich man was accustomed to honor a sufi
by giving him pieces of silver.

"Would you like *one* piece of silver now,
O Lord of my Spirit, or *three* at breakfast
tomorrow morning?"
                            The sufi answered,
"I love the half a coin that I have already in my hand
from yesterday more than the promise of a whole one

today, or the promise of a hundred tomorrow.
A sufi is the child of *this* moment."

Back to the mouse, who says,
                              "The slap of Now
has cash in its hand. Give me slaps,
on the neck, anywhere!"

Soul of my soul of the soul of a hundred universes,
be water in this now-river, so jasmine flowers
will lift on the brim, and someone far off
can notice the flower-colors and know
there's water here.

"The sign is in the face." You can look at an orchard
and tell if it rained last night. That freshness
is the sign.

Again, the mouse,
                              "Friend, I'm made from the ground,
and for the ground. You're of the water.

I'm always standing on the bank calling to you.
Have mercy. I can't follow you into the water.
Isn't there some way we can be in touch?
A messenger? Some reminder?"

The two friends decided that the answer
was a long, a *longing!* string, with one end tied
to the mouse's foot and the other to the frog's,
so that by pulling on it their secret connection
might be remembered and the two could meet,
as the soul does with the body.

The froglike soul often escapes from the body
and soars in the happy water. Then the mouse body
pulls on the string, and the soul thinks,
                              Damn.
I have to go back on the riverbank and talk
with that scatterbrained mouse!
                              You'll hear more about this
when you really wake up, on Resurrection Day!

So the mouse and the frog tied the string,
even though the frog had a hunch some tangling
was to come.

        Never ignore those intuitions.
When you feel some slight repugnance about doing something,
listen to it. These premonitions come from God.

Remember the story of the military elephant
who would not move toward the Kaaba. Paralyzed
in that direction, yet swift if pointed toward Yemen.
It had some in-knowing from the unseen.

So the prophet Jacob, when his other sons wanted
to take Joseph out in the country for two days,
had a heart-sickness about their going, and it was true,
though divine destiny prevailed, despite his foreboding,
as it will.

        It's not always a blind man
who falls in a pit. Sometimes it's one who can see.

A holy one does sometimes fall,
but by that tribulation, he or she ascends,
escapes many illusions, escapes
conventional religion, escapes
being so bound to phenomena.

Think of how PHENOMENA come trooping
out of the desert of non-existence
into this materiality.

        Morning and night,
they arrive in a long line and take over
from each other, "It's my turn now. Get out!"

A son comes of age, and the father packs up.
This place of phenomena is a wide exchange
of highways, with everything going all sorts
of different ways.

        We seem to be sitting still,
but we're actually moving, and the fantasies
of phenomena are sliding through us
like ideas through curtains.

        They go to the well

of deep love inside each of us.
They fill their jars there, and they leave.

There is a source they come from,
and a fountain inside here.
                              Be generous.
Be grateful. Confess when you're not.

We can't know
what the divine intelligence
has in mind!

Who am I,
standing in the midst of this
thought-traffic?

THE FORCE OF FRIENDSHIP

A sea cow, a dugong, finds a special pearl
and brings it up on land at night. By the light it gives off
the dugong can graze on hyacinths and lilies.

The excrement of the dugong is precious ambergris
because it eats such beauty. Anyone who feeds on majesty
becomes eloquent. The bee, from mystic inspiration,
fills its rooms with honey.

So the dugong grazes at night in the pearl-glow.
Presently, a merchant comes and drops black loam
over the pearl, then hides behind a tree to watch.

The dugong surges about the meadow like a blind bull.
Twenty times it rushes at nothing, passing the mound
where the pearl is.
                        So Satan couldn't see
the spirit center inside Adam.
                              God says, *Descend,*
and a huge pearl from Aden gets buried under dirt.
The merchant knows,
                        but the dugong doesn't.

Every clay-pile with a pearl inside
loves to be near any other clay-pile with a pearl,
but those without pearls cannot stand to be near
the hidden companionship.

Remember the mouse on the riverbank?
There's a love-string stretching into the water
hoping for the frog.
                 Suddenly a raven grips the mouse
and flies off. The frog too, from the riverbottom,
with one foot tangled in invisible string,
follows, suspended in the air.
               Amazed faces ask,
"When did a raven ever go underwater
                    and catch a frog?"

The frog answers,
          This is the force of Friendship.
What draws friends together
does not conform to laws of nature.
Form doesn't know about spiritual closeness.
If a grain of barley approaches a grain of wheat,
an ant must be carrying it. A black ant on black felt.
You can't see it, but if grains go toward each other,
it's there.
        A hand shifts our birdcages around.
Some are brought closer. Some move apart.
Do not try to reason it out. Be conscious
of who draws you and who not.

Gabriel was always there with Jesus, lifting him
above the dark-blue vault, the night-fortress world,
just as the raven of longing carries the flying frog.

THE VIGIL

Don't go to sleep one night.
What you most want will come to you then.
Warmed by a sun inside, you'll see wonders.

Tonight, don't put your head down.
Be tough, and strength will come.
That which adoration adores
appears at night. Those asleep
may miss it. One night Moses stayed awake
and asked, and saw a light in a tree.

Then he walked at night for ten years,
until finally he saw the whole tree
illuminated. Muhammad rode his horse
through the nightsky. The day is for work.
The night for love. Don't let someone
bewitch you. Some people sleep at night.

But not lovers. They sit in the dark
and talk to God, who told David,
Those who sleep all night every night
and claim to be connected to us, they lie.

Lovers can't sleep when they feel the privacy
of the beloved all around them. Someone
who's thirsty may sleep for a little while,
but he or she will dream of water, a full jar
beside a creek, or the spiritual water you get
from another person. All night, listen
to the conversation. Stay up.
This moment is all there is.

Death will take it away soon enough.
You'll be gone, and this earth will be left
without a sweetheart, nothing but weeds
growing inside thorns.

I'm through. Read the rest of this poem
in the dark tonight.
                              Do I have a head? And feet?

Shams, so loved by Tabrizians, I close my lips.
I wait for you to come and open them.

TWO FRIENDS

A certain person came to the Friend's door
and knocked.
                    "Who's there?"
"It's me."

The Friend answered, "Go away. There's no place
for raw meat at this table."

The individual went wandering for a year.
Nothing but the fire of separation
can change hypocrisy and ego. The person returned
completely cooked,
walked up and down in front of the Friend's house,
gently knocked.
                    "Who is it?"

"You."

"Please come in, my self,
there's no place in this house for two.
The doubled end of the thread is not what goes through
the eye of the needle.
It's a single-pointed, fined-down, thread end,
not a big ego-beast with baggage."

But how can a camel be thinned to a thread?
With the shears of practices, with *doing* things.

And with help from the one who brings
impossibilities to pass, who quiets willfulness,
who gives sight to one blind from birth.

Every day that one does something.
Take that as your text.

Every day God sends forth three powerful energies:
One, from the sperm of the father into the mother,
so growth may begin.
Two, a birth from the womb of the ground,
so male and female may spring into existence.

Three, there's a surge up from the surface
into what is beyond dying, that the real beauty
of creating can be recognized.

There's no way to ever say this.

Let's return to the two friends whose thread
became single,
     who spell with their two letters
the original word,

                    BE.

B and *E* tighten around subjects and objects
that one knot may hold them. Two scissor blades
make one cut.
                    And watch two men washing clothes.
One makes dry clothes wet. The other makes
wet clothes dry. They seem to be thwarting each other,
but their work is a perfect harmony.

Every holy person seems to have a different doctrine
and practice, but there's really only one work.

Someone listening to a millstone falls asleep.
No matter. The stone keeps turning.

Water from the mountain
far above the mill keeps flowing down.
The sleepers will get their bread.

Underground it moves, without sound, and without
repetition. Show us where that source of speech is
that has no alphabet. That spaciousness.

Where we are now is a narrow fantasy
that comes from there, and the actual, outside world
is even narrower. Narrowness is pain,
and the cause of narrowness is manyness.

Creation was spoken with one sound, BE.
The two letters, *B* and *E,*
                    to record it,

came after.
                    The meaning of the sound
and its resonance
                    are one.

There's no way to ever say this,
in so many words! And no place
to stop saying it.

Meanwhile, a lion and a wolf were fighting. . . .

THE SERVANT WHO LOVED HIS PRAYERS

At dawn a certain rich man
wanted to go to the steambaths.
He woke his servant, Sunqur,
                    "Ho! Get moving! Get the basin
and the towels and the clay for washing
and let's go to the baths."

Sunqur immediately collected what was needed,
and they set out side by side along the road.

As they passed the mosque, the call to prayer sounded.
Sunqur loved his five-times prayer.
                              "Please, master,
rest on this bench for a while that I may recite sura 98,
which begins,
                    'You who treat your slave with kindness.'"

The master sat on the bench outside while Sunqur went in.
When prayers were over, and the priest and all the worshipers
had left, still Sunqur remained inside. The master waited
and waited. Finally he yelled into the mosque,
                                        "Sunqur,
why don't you come out?"
                    "I can't. This clever one
won't let me. Have a little more patience.
I hear you out there."
                    Seven times the master waited,

and then shouted. Sunqur's reply was always the same,
"Not yet. He won't let me come out yet."

> "But there's no one

in there but you. Everyone else has left.
Who makes you sit still so long?"

"The one who keeps me in here is the one
who keeps you out there.
The same who will not let you in will not let me out."

The ocean will not allow its fish out of itself.
Nor does it let land animals in
where the subtle and delicate fish move.

The land creatures lumber along on the ground.
No cleverness can change this. There's only one
opener for the lock of these matters.

Forget your figuring. Forget your self. Listen to your Friend.
When you become totally obedient to that one,
you'll be free.

IMRA'U 'L-QAYS

Imra'u 'l-Qays, King of the Arabs,
was very handsome, and a poet, full of love songs.

Women loved him desperately.
Everyone loved him, but there came one night
an experience that changed him completely.
He left his kingdom and his family.
He put on dervish robes and wandered
from one weather, one landscape, to another.

Love dissolved his king-self
and led him to Tabuk, where he worked for a time
making bricks. Someone told the King of Tabuk
about Imra'u 'l-Qays, and that king went to visit him
at night.

> "King of the Arabs, handsome Joseph of this age,
ruler of two empires, one composed of territories,

and the other of the beauty of women,
if you would consent to stay with me,
I would be honored. You abandon kingdoms,
because you want more than kingdoms."

The King of Tabuk went on like this,
praising Imra'u 'l-Qays, and talking theology
and philosophy. Imra'u 'l-Qays kept silent.
Then suddenly he leaned and whispered something
in the second king's ear, and that second, that
second king became a wanderer too.

They walked out of town hand in hand.
No royal belts, no thrones.

This is what love does and continues to do.

It tastes like honey to adults and milk to children.
Love is the last thirty-pound bale.
When you load it on, the boat tips over.

So they wandered around China like birds
pecking at bits of grain. They rarely spoke
because of the dangerous seriousness
of the secret they knew.

That love-secret spoken pleasantly, or in irritation,
severs a hundred thousand heads in one swing.
A love-lion grazes in the soul's pasture,
while the scimitar of this secret approaches.
It's a killing better than any living.

All that world-power wants, really,
is this weakness.

So these kings talked in low tones,
and carefully. Only God knows what they said.

They used unsayable words. Bird language.
But some people have imitated them, learned
a few birdcalls, and gotten prestigious.

Don't unstring the bow.
I am your four-feathered arrow
that has not been used yet.

I am a strong knifeblade word,
not some *if* or *maybe,*
dissolving in air.

I am sunlight slicing the dark.
Who made this night?
A forge deep in the earth-mud.

What is the body?
Endurance.

What is love?
Gratitude.

What is hidden
in our chests?
Laughter.

What else?
Compassion.

Let the beloved be a hat pulled down firmly on my head.
Or drawstrings pulled and tied around my chest.

Someone asks, How does love have hands and feet?
Love is the sprouting bed for hands and feet!

Your father and mother were playing love games.
They came together, and you appeared!

Don't ask what love can make or do!
Look at the colors of the world.

The riverwater moving in all rivers at once.
The truth that lives in Shams' face.

THE BLOCKED ROAD

I wish I knew what you wanted.
You block the road and won't give me rest.
You pull my lead-rope one way, then the other.
You act cold, my darling!
Do you hear what I say?

Will this night of talking ever end?
Why am I still embarrassed and timid about you?
You are thousands. You are one.
Quiet, but most articulate.

Your name is Spring.
Your name is wine.
Your name is the nausea
that comes from wine!

You are my doubting
and the lightpoints
in my eyes.

You are every image, and yet
I'm homesick for you.

Can I get there?
Where the deer pounces on the lion,
where the one I'm after's
after me?

This drum and these words keep pounding!
Let them both smash through their coverings
into silence.

A BABBLING CHILD

If my words are not saying what you would say,
slap my face. Discipline me as a loving mother does
a babbling child caught up in nonsense.

A thirsty man runs into the sea, and the sea
holds a sword to his throat.

A lily looks at a bank of roses
and wilts and says nothing.

I am a tambourine. Don't put me aside
till the fast dancing starts.
Play me some all along.
Help me with these little sounds.

Joseph is most beautiful when he's completely naked,
but his shirt gives you an idea,
as the body lets you glimpse the glitter
on the water of the soul.

Even if the corpse washer binds my jaw shut,
you'll still hear this song
coming out of my dead-silence.

※

Who sees inside from outside?
Who finds hundreds of mysteries
even where minds are deranged?

See through his eyes what he sees.
Who then is looking out from his eyes?

※

CONSTANT CONVERSATION

Who is luckiest in this whole orchestra? The reed.
Its mouth touches your lips to learn music.
All reeds, sugarcane especially, think only
of this chance. They sway in the canebrakes,
free in the many ways they dance.

Without you the instruments would die.
One sits close beside you. Another takes a long kiss.
The tambourine begs, *Touch my skin so I can be myself.*
Let me feel you enter each limb bone by bone,
that what died last night can be whole today.

Why live some soberer way and feel you ebbing out?
I won't do it.
Either give me enough wine or leave me alone,
now that I know how it is
to be with you in a constant conversation.

BONFIRE AT MIDNIGHT

A shout comes out of my room
where I've been cooped up.
After all my lust and dead living I can still live with you.
You want me to.
You fix and bring me food.
You forget the way I've been.

The ocean moves and surges in the heat
of the middle of the day,
in the heat of this thought I'm having.
Why aren't all human resistances burning up with this thought?

It's a drum and arms waving.
It's a bonfire at midnight on the top edge of a hill,
this meeting again with you.

IN BETWEEN STORIES

Turn from the ocean now
toward dry land.

When you're with children, talk about toys.
From playthings, little by little, they reach
into deeper wisdom and clarity. Gradually,
they lose interest in their toys.

They have a sense of wholeness in them already.
If they were completely demented,
they wouldn't play at all.
                              Did you hear that?
It's the man who was looking for treasure.

He wants me to finish his story.

                              You didn't hear him?
Then he must be inside me yelling, "Over here!
Come over here!"

                    Don't think of him as a seeker, though.
Whatever he's looking for, he is that himself.
How can a lover be anything but the beloved?

Every second he's bowing into a mirror.
If he could see for just a second one molecule
of what's there without fantasizing about it,
he'd explode.

                    His imagination, and he himself,
would vanish, with all his knowledge, obliterated
into a new birth, a perfectly clear view,
a voice that says, *I am God.*

That same voice told the angels to bow to Adam,
because they were identical with Adam.

It's the voice that first said,
There is no Reality but God.
There is only God.

                    Husam pulls me by the ear now,
"Wash your mouth! By trying to say these things,
you conceal them. Just finish telling the story
about the dervish who was looking for treasure.

Your listeners love difficulties, not unity!
Talk about world troubles.
Don't distribute water from the fountain.
They don't want that.

                         In fact, they've loaded themselves
with dirt clods to clog up the fountain.
They'd like to shut it off!"

We are listeners as well as speakers
of this mystery, both of us,
but who else will join
this strange companionship?

That's what Husam wants to know!

One dervish to another, *What was your vision of God's presence?*
I haven't seen anything.
But for the sake of conversation, I'll tell you a story.

God's presence is there in front of me, a fire on the left,
a lovely stream on the right.
One group walks toward the fire, *into* the fire, another
toward the sweet flowing water.
No one knows which are blessed and which not.
Whoever walks into the fire appears suddenly in the stream.
A head goes under on the water surface, that head
pokes out of the fire.
Most people guard against going into the fire,
and so end up in it.
Those who love the water of pleasure and make it their devotion
are cheated with this reversal.
The trickery goes further.
The voice of the fire tells the *truth* saying, *I am not fire.*
I am fountainhead. Come into me and don't mind the sparks.

If you are a friend of God, fire is your water.
You should wish to have a hundred thousand sets of mothwings,
so you could burn them away, one set a night.
The moth sees light and goes into fire. You should see fire
and go toward light. Fire is what of God is world-consuming.
Water, world-protecting.
Somehow each gives the appearance of the other. To these eyes
you have now, what looks like water
burns. What looks like fire
is a great relief to be inside.
You've seen a magician make a bowl of rice
seem a dish full of tiny, live worms.
Before an assembly with one breath he made the floor swarm
with scorpions that weren't there.
How much more amazing God's tricks.
Generation after generation lies down, defeated, they think,
but they're like a woman underneath a man, circling him.
One molecule-mote-second thinking of God's reversal

of comfort and pain is better
than any attending ritual. That splinter
of intelligence is substance.

The fire and water themselves:
accidental, done with mirrors.

THE MUSIC

For sixty years I have been forgetful,
every minute, but not for a second
has this flowing toward me stopped or slowed.
I deserve nothing. Today I recognize
that I am the guest the mystics talk about.
I play this living music for my host.
Everything today is for the host.

~

I saw you last night in the gathering,
but could not take you openly in my arms,

so I put my lips next to your cheek,
pretending to talk privately.

~

THE TENT

Outside, the freezing desert night.
This other night inside grows warm, kindling.
Let the landscape be covered with thorny crust.
We have a soft garden in here.
The continents blasted,
cities and little towns, everything
become a scorched, blackened ball.

The news we hear is full of grief for that future,
but the real news inside here
is there's no news at all.

⤜

Friend, our closeness is this:
anywhere you put your foot, feel me
in the firmness under you.

How is it with this love,
I see your world and not you?

⤜

Listen to presences inside poems,
Let them take you where they will.

Follow those private hints,
and never leave the premises.

8 ⚡ Being a Lover: The Sunrise Ruby

ON BEING A LOVER

Being a lover is close to being a worker. When the ruby becomes the sunrise, its transparency changes to a daily discipline. There's a story about a sufi who rips his robe and gives it the name faraji, *which means "ripped open" or "happiness" or "one who brings the joy of being opened." It comes from the stem* faraj, *which also refers to the genitals, male and female. The sufi's teacher sees the purity of the name and the action, while others notice only his ragged appearance. Peace and compassion come as coverings are thrown open and the streaming beauty of emotion flows through the lover-worker. Rumi suggests in another poem that being human is a guest house where travelers are welcomed and entertained. The work is to be a good host at the caravanserai.*

THE SUNRISE RUBY

In the early morning hour,
just before dawn, lover and beloved wake
and take a drink of water.

She asks, "Do you love me or yourself more?
Really, tell the absolute truth."

He says, "There's nothing left of *me*.
I'm like a ruby held up to the sunrise.
Is it still a stone, or a world
made of redness? It has no resistance
to sunlight."

This is how Hallaj said, *I am God,*
and told the truth!

The ruby and the sunrise are one.
Be courageous and discipline yourself.

Completely become hearing and ear,
and wear this sun-ruby as an earring.

Work. Keep digging your well.
Don't think about getting off from work.
Water is there somewhere.

Submit to a daily practice.
Your loyalty to that
is a ring on the door.

Keep knocking, and the joy inside
will eventually open a window
and look out to see who's there.

WATER FROM YOUR SPRING

What was in that candle's light
that opened and consumed me so quickly?

Come back, my friend! The form of our love
is not a created form.

Nothing can help me but that beauty.
There was a dawn I remember

when my soul heard something
from your soul. I drank water

from your spring and felt
the current take me.

YOU SWEEP THE FLOOR

The lord of beauty enters the soul
as a man walks into an orchard
in Spring.
            Come into me
that way again!
                Light the lamp
in the eye of Joseph. Cure Jacob's
sadness. Though you never left,
come and sit down here and ask,
"Why are you so confused?"

Like a fresh idea in an artist's mind,
you fashion things before they come into being.

You sweep the floor like the man
who keeps the doorway.
                    When you brush
a form clean, it becomes
what it truly is.

You guard your silence perfectly
like a waterbag that doesn't leak.

You live where Shams lives,
because your heart-donkey was strong enough
to take you there.

EACH NOTE

Advice doesn't help lovers!
They're not the kind of mountain stream
you can build a dam across.

An intellectual doesn't know
what the drunk is feeling!

Don't try to figure
what those lost inside love
will do next!

Someone in charge would give up all his power,
if he caught one whiff of the wine-musk
from the room where the lovers
are doing who-knows-what!

One of them tries to dig a hole through a mountain.
One flees from academic honors.
One laughs at famous mustaches!

Life freezes if it doesn't get a taste
of this almond cake.
                    The stars come up spinning
every night, bewildered in love.
                        They'd grow tired
with that revolving, if they weren't.
                        They'd say,
"How long do we have to *do* this!"

God picks up the reed-flute world and blows.
Each note is a need coming through one of us,
a passion, a longing-pain.
                        Remember the lips
where the wind-breath originated,
and let your note be clear.
Don't try to end it.
Be your note.
I'll show you how it's enough.

Go up on the roof at night
in this city of the soul.

Let *everyone* climb on their roofs
and sing their notes!

Sing loud!

GRANITE AND WINEGLASS

You are granite.
I am an empty wineglass.

You know what happens when we touch!
You laugh like the sun coming up laughs
at a star that disappears into it.

Love opens my chest, and thought
returns to its confines.

Patience and rational considerations leave.
Only passion stays, whimpering and feverish.

Some men fall down in the road like dregs thrown out.
Then, totally reckless, the next morning

they gallop out with new purposes. Love
is the reality, and poetry is the drum

that calls us to that. Don't keep complaining
about loneliness! Let the fear-language of that theme

crack open and float away. Let the priest come down
from his tower, and not go back up!

BUOYANCY

Love has taken away my practices
and filled me with poetry.

I tried to keep quietly repeating,
No strength but yours,
but I couldn't.

I had to clap and sing.
I used to be respectable and chaste and stable,
but who can stand in this strong wind
and remember those things?

A mountain keeps an echo deep inside itself.
That's how I hold your voice.

I am scrap wood thrown in your fire,
and quickly reduced to smoke.

I saw you and became empty.
This emptiness, more beautiful than existence,
it obliterates existence, and yet when it comes,
existence thrives and creates more existence!

The sky is blue. The world is a blind man
squatting on the road.

But whoever sees your emptiness
sees beyond blue and beyond the blind man.

A great soul hides like Muhammad, or Jesus,
moving through a crowd in a city
where no one knows him.

To praise is to praise
how one surrenders
to the emptiness.

To praise the sun is to praise your own eyes.
Praise, the ocean. What we say, a little ship.

So the sea-journey goes on, and who knows where!
Just to be held by the ocean is the best luck
we could have. It's a total waking up!

Why should we grieve that we've been sleeping?
It doesn't matter how long we've been unconscious.

We're groggy, but let the guilt go.
Feel the motions of tenderness
around you, the buoyancy.

MUSIC MASTER

You that love lovers,
this is your home. Welcome!

In the midst of making form, love
made this form that melts form,
with love for the door,
soul the vestibule.

Watch the dust grains moving
in the light near the window.

Their dance is our dance.

We rarely hear the inward music,
but we're all dancing to it nevertheless,

directed by the one who teaches us,
the pure joy of the sun,
our music master.

❧

When I am with you, we stay up all night.
When you're not here, I can't go to sleep.

Praise God for these two insomnias!
And the difference between them.

❧

The minute I heard my first love story
I started looking for you, not knowing
how blind that was.

Lovers don't finally meet somewhere.
They're in each other all along.

❧

We are the mirror as well as the face in it.
We are tasting the taste this minute
of eternity. We are pain
and what cures pain, both. We are
the sweet cold water and the jar that pours.

❧

I want to hold you close like a lute,
so we can cry out with loving.

You would rather throw stones at a mirror?
I am your mirror, and here are the stones.

SOMEONE DIGGING IN THE GROUND

An eye is meant to see things.
The soul is here for its own joy.
A head has one use: for loving a true love.
Legs: to run after.

Love is for vanishing into the sky. The mind,
for learning what men have done and tried to do.
Mysteries are not to be solved. The eye goes blind
when it only wants to see *why*.

A lover is always accused of something.
But when he finds his love, whatever was lost
in the looking comes back completely changed.
On the way to Mecca, many dangers: thieves,
the blowing sand, only camel's milk to drink.
Still each pilgrim kisses the black stone there
with pure longing, feeling in the surface
the taste of the lips he wants.

This talk is like stamping new coins. They pile up,
while the real work is done outside
by someone digging in the ground.

Learn about your inner self from those who know such things,
but don't repeat verbatim what they say.
Zuleikha let everything be the name of Joseph, from celery seed
to aloes wood. She loved him so much she concealed his name
in many different phrases, the inner meanings
known only to her. When she said, *The wax is softening
near the fire,* she meant, My love is wanting me.
Or if she said, *Look, the moon is up* or *The willow has new leaves*
or *The branches are trembling* or *The coriander seeds
have caught fire* or *The roses are opening*
or *The king is in a good mood today* or *Isn't that lucky?*
or *The furniture needs dusting* or
The water carrier is here or *It's almost daylight* or
These vegetables are perfect or *The bread needs more salt*
or *The clouds seem to be moving against the wind*
or *My head hurts* or *My headache's better,*
anything she praises, it's Joseph's touch she means,
any complaint, it's his being away.
When she's hungry, it's for him. Thirsty, his name is a sherbet.
Cold, he's a fur. This is what the Friend can do
when one is in such love. Sensual people use the holy names
often, but they don't work for them.
The miracle Jesus did by being the name of God,
Zuleikha felt in the name of *Joseph.*

When one is united to the core of another, to speak of that
is to breathe the name *Hu,* empty of self and filled
with love. As the saying goes, *The pot drips what is in it.*
The saffron spice of connecting, laughter.
The onion smell of separation, crying.
Others have many things and people they love.
This is not the way of Friend and friend.

THE GUEST HOUSE

This being human is a guest house.
Every morning a new arrival.

A joy, a depression, a meanness,
some momentary awareness comes
as an unexpected visitor.

Welcome and entertain them all!
Even if they're a crowd of sorrows,
who violently sweep your house
empty of its furniture,
still, treat each guest honorably.
He may be clearing you out
for some new delight.

The dark thought, the shame, the malice,
meet them at the door laughing,
and invite them in.

Be grateful for whoever comes,
because each has been sent
as a guide from beyond.

9 ✍ The Pickaxe:
Getting to the Treasure Beneath the Foundation

ON THE PICKAXE

One view of identity is that it's a structure made of what we identify with. Rumi says that identity must be torn down, completely demolished along with its little tailoring shop, the patch-sewing of eating and drinking consolations. Inner work is not all ecstatic surrender. Don't listen too often, Rumi advises, to the comforting part of the self that gives you what you want. Pray instead for a tough instructor. Nothing less than the radical disassembling of what we've wanted and gotten, and what we still wish for, allows us to discover the value of true being that lies underneath. The pickaxe, for Rumi, represents whatever does this fierce attention-work: clear discernment, a teacher's presence, simple strength, and honesty with oneself. The pickaxe dismantles the illusory personality and finds two glints in the dirt. Like eyes they are, but these jewel lights are not personal. Rumi points to a treasure within our lives unconnected to experience. It is intrinsic, beyond calculation, a given, reached after the ego is cleared away and a one-pointedness digs under the premises.

WHO MAKES THESE CHANGES?

Who makes these changes?
I shoot an arrow right.
It lands left.
I ride after a deer and find myself
chased by a hog.
I plot to get what I want
and end up in prison.

I dig pits to trap others
and fall in.

I should be suspicious
of what I want.

WHY WINE IS FORBIDDEN

When the Prophet's ray of intelligence
struck the dim-witted man he was with,
the man got very happy, and talkative.

Soon, he began unmannerly raving.
This is the problem with a selflessness
that comes quickly,
                              as with wine.
If the wine drinker
has a deep gentleness in him,
he will show that,
                        when drunk.
But if he has hidden anger and arrogance,
those appear,
                        and since most people do,
wine is forbidden to everyone.

ON RESURRECTION DAY

On Resurrection Day your body testifies against you.
Your hand says, "I stole money."
Your lips, "I said meanness."
Your feet, "I went where I shouldn't."
Your genitals, "Me too."

They will make your praying sound hypocritical.
Let the body's doings speak openly now,
without your saying a word,
as a student's walking behind a teacher
says, "This one knows more clearly
than I the way."

This place is a dream.
Only a sleeper considers it real.

Then death comes like dawn,
and you wake up laughing
at what you thought was your grief.

But there's a difference with *this* dream.
Everything cruel and unconscious
done in the illusion of the present world,
all that does not fade away at the death-waking.

It stays,
and it must be *interpreted*.

All the mean laughing,
all the quick, sexual wanting,
those torn coats of Joseph,
they change into powerful wolves
that you must face.

The retaliation that sometimes comes now,
the swift, payback hit,
is just a boy's game
to what the other will be.

You know about circumcision here.
It's full castration there!

And this groggy time we live,
this is what it's like:

        A man goes to sleep in the town
where he has always lived, and he dreams he's living
in another town.

        In the dream, he doesn't remember
the town he's sleeping in his bed in. He believes
the reality of the dream town.

The world is that kind of sleep.

The dust of many crumbled cities
settles over us like a forgetful doze,

but we are older than those cities.

We began
as a mineral. We emerged into plant life
and into the animal state, and then into being human,
and always we have forgotten our former states,
except in early spring when we slightly recall
being green again.

That's how a young person turns
toward a teacher. That's how a baby leans
toward the breast, without knowing the secret
of its desire, yet turning instinctively.

Humankind is being led along an evolving course,
through this migration of intelligences,
and though we seem to be sleeping,
there is an inner wakefulness
that directs the dream,

and that will eventually startle us back
to the truth of who we are.

THE PICKAXE

Some commentary on *I was a hidden treasure,*
and I desired to be known: tear down

this house. A hundred thousand new houses
can be built from the transparent yellow carnelian

buried beneath it, and the only way to get to that
is to do the work of demolishing and then

digging under the foundations. With that value
in hand all the new construction will be done

without effort. And anyway, sooner or later this house
will fall on its own. The jewel treasure will be

uncovered, but it won't be yours then. The buried
wealth is your pay for doing the demolition,

the pick and shovel work. If you wait and just
let it happen, you'd bite your hand and say,

"I didn't do as I knew I should have." This
is a rented house. You don't own the deed.

You have a lease, and you've set up a little shop,
where you barely make a living sewing patches

on torn clothing. Yet only a few feet underneath
are two veins, pure red and bright gold carnelian.

Quick! Take the pickaxe and pry the foundation.
You've got to quit this seamstress work.

What does the patch-sewing *mean,* you ask. Eating
and drinking. The heavy cloak of the body

is always getting torn. You patch it with food,
and other restless ego-satisfactions. Rip up

one board from the shop floor and look into
the basement. You'll see two glints in the dirt.

ZIKR

A naked man jumps in the river, hornets swarming
above him. The water is the *zikr,* remembering,
There is no reality but God. There is only God.

The hornets are his sexual remembering, this woman,
that woman. Or if a woman, this man, that.
The head comes up. They sting.

Breathe water. Become river head to foot.
Hornets leave you alone then. Even if you're far
from the river, they pay no attention.

No one looks for stars when the sun's out.
A person blended into God does not disappear. He, or she,
is just completely soaked in God's qualities.
Do you need a quote from the Qur'an?

All shall be brought into our Presence.

Join those travelers. The lamps we burn go out,
some quickly. Some last till daybreak.
Some are dim, some intense, all fed with fuel.

If a light goes out in one house, that doesn't affect
the next house. This is the story of the animal soul,
not the divine soul. The sun shines on every house.
When it goes down, all houses get dark.

Light is the image of your teacher. Your enemies
love the dark. A spider weaves a web over a light,
out of himself, or herself, makes a veil.

Don't try to control a wild horse by grabbing its leg.
Take hold the neck. Use a bridle. Be sensible.
Then ride! There is a need for self-denial.

Don't be contemptuous of old obediences. They help.

THE CORE OF MASCULINITY

The core of masculinity does not derive
from being male,
nor friendliness from those who console.

Your old grandmother says, "Maybe you shouldn't
go to school. You look a little pale."

Run when you hear that.
A father's stern slaps are better.

Your bodily soul wants comforting.
The severe father wants spiritual clarity.

He scolds but eventually
leads you into the open.

Pray for a tough instructor
to hear and act and stay within you.

We have been busy accumulating solace.
Make us afraid of how we were.

🔖

I honor those who try
to rid themselves of any lying,
who empty the self
and have only clear being there.

🔖

DERVISH AT THE DOOR

A dervish knocked at a house
to ask for a piece of dry bread,
or moist, it didn't matter.

"This is not a bakery," said the owner.

"Might you have a bit of gristle then?"

"Does this look like a butchershop?"

"A little flour?"

"Do you hear a grinding stone?"

"Some water?"

"This is not a well."

Whatever the dervish asked for,
the man made some tired joke
and refused to give him anything.

Finally the dervish ran in the house,
lifted his robe, and squatted
as though to take a shit.

"Hey, hey!"

"Quiet, you sad man. A deserted place
is a fine spot to relieve oneself,
and since there's no living thing here,
or means of living, it needs fertilizing."

The dervish began his own list
of questions and answers.

"What kind of bird are you? Not a falcon,
trained for the royal hand. Not a peacock,
painted with everyone's eyes. Not a parrot,
that talks for sugar cubes. Not a nightingale,
that sings like someone in love.

Not a hoopoe bringing messages to Solomon,
or a stork that builds on a cliffside.

What exactly do you do?
You are no known species.

You haggle and make jokes
to keep what you own for yourself.

You have forgotten the One
who doesn't care about ownership,
who doesn't try to turn a profit
from every human exchange."

10 ⨞ Art as Flirtation with Surrender: Wanting New Silk Harp Strings

ON FLIRTATION

The design on the curtains is not what they conceal. Artists love shapes for enclosure, the chained cup beside the waterfall as a way of tasting the waterfall and maybe even the presence of someone meditating in the cave behind it. Forms keep splitting their chrysali, but the old harper wants one more set of silk strings. Some sufis have seen the beauties of art as something that can slow down soul growth. Art gives a teasing taste of surrender without the full experience. Beautiful poetry can keep one on the verge of the oceanic annihilation in God. Rumi says, we've been walking in the surf holding our robes up, when we should be diving naked under, and deeper under.

OMAR AND THE OLD POET

The harper had grown old. His voice was choked sounding
and harsh, and some of his harp strings were broken.

He went to the graveyard at Medina and wept. "Lord,
you've always accepted counterfeit coins from me!
Take these prayers again, and give me enough
to buy new silk strings for my harp."

He put the harp down for a pillow and went to sleep.
The bird of his soul escaped! Free of the body
and the grieving, flying in a vast simple region
that was itself, where it could sing its truth.

"I love this having no head, this tasting without mouth,
this memory without regret, how without hands I gather

rose and basil on an infinitely stretching-out plain
that is my joy." So this waterbird plunged into its ocean,

Job's fountain where Job was healed of all afflictions,
the pure sunrise. If this *Mathnawi* were suddenly sky,
it could not hold half the mystery that this old poet
was enjoying in sleep. If there were a clear way
into that, no one would stay here!

The Caliph Omar, meanwhile, was napping nearby,
and a voice came, "Give seven hundred gold dinars
to the man sleeping in the cemetery."

Everyone understands this voice when it comes.
It speaks with the same authority to Turk and Kurd,
Persian, Arab, Ethiopian, one language!

Omar went to the place and sat by the sleeping man.
Omar sneezed, and the poet sprang up thinking
this great man was there to accuse him.

"No. Sit here beside me. I have a secret to tell you.
There is gold enough in this sack to buy new silk
strings for your instrument. Take it,
buy them, and come back here."

The old poet heard and realized the generosity
that had come. He threw the harp on the ground
and broke it. "These songs, breath by breath,

have kept me minding the musical modes of Iraq
and the rhythms of Persia. The minor *zirafgand,*
the liquid freshness of the twenty-four melodies,

these have distracted me while caravan after caravan
was leaving! My poems have kept me in my self,
which was the greatest gift to me, that now
I surrender back."

When someone is counting out
gold for you, don't look at your hands,
or the gold. Look at the giver.

"But even this wailing recrimination," said Omar,
"is just another shape for enclosure, another joint
on the reed. Pierce the segments and be hollow,
with perforated walls, so flute music can happen.

Don't be a searcher wrapped in the importance of his quest.
Repent of your repenting!" The old man's heart
woke, no longer in love with treble
and bass, without weeping

or laughter. In the true bewilderment of the soul
he went out beyond any seeking, beyond words
and telling, drowned in the beauty,
drowned beyond deliverance.

Waves cover the old man.

Nothing more can be said of him.

He has shaken out his robe,
and there's nothing in it anymore.

There is a chase where a falcon dives into the forest
and doesn't come back up. Every moment,
the sunlight is totally empty
and totally full.

AN EGYPT THAT DOESN'T EXIST

I want to say words that flame
as I say them, but I keep quiet and don't try
to make both worlds fit in one mouthful.

I keep secret in myself an Egypt
that doesn't exist.
Is that good or bad? I don't know.

For years I gave away sexual love
with my eyes. Now I don't.
I'm not in any one place. I don't have a name
for what I give away. Whatever Shams
gave, that you can have from me.

The Prophet said, "There are some who see me
by the same light in which I am seeing them.
Our natures are one.
                        Without reference to any strands
of lineage, without reference to texts or traditions,
we drink the life-water together."
                                  Here's a story
about that hidden mystery:
                           The Chinese and the Greeks
were arguing as to who were the better artists.
The king said,
               "We'll settle this matter with a debate."
The Chinese began talking,
but the Greeks wouldn't say anything.
They left.
            The Chinese suggested then
that they each be given a room to work on
with their artistry, two rooms facing each other
and divided by a curtain.
                       The Chinese asked the king
for a hundred colors, all the variations,
and each morning they came to where
the dyes were kept and took them all.
The Greeks took no colors.
"They're not part of our work."
                       They went to their room
and began cleaning and polishing the walls. All day
every day they made those walls as pure and clear
as an open sky.
            There is a way that leads from all-colors
to colorlessness. Know that the magnificent variety
of the clouds and the weather comes from
the total simplicity of the sun and the moon.

The Chinese finished, and they were so happy.
They beat the drums in the joy of completion.

The king entered their room,
astonished by the gorgeous color and detail.

The Greeks then pulled the curtain dividing the rooms.
The Chinese figures and images shimmeringly reflected
on the clear Greek walls. They lived there,
even more beautifully, and always
changing in the light.

The Greek art is the sufi way.
They don't study books of philosophical thought.

They make their loving clearer and clearer.
No wantings, no anger. In that purity
they receive and reflect the images of every moment,
from here, from the stars, from the void.

They take them in
as though they were seeing
with the lighted clarity
that sees them.

ᨘ

In your light I learn how to love.
In your beauty, how to make poems.

You dance inside my chest,
where no one sees you,

but sometimes I do,
and that sight becomes this art.

ᨘ

Drumsound rises on the air,
its throb, my heart.

A voice inside the beat says,
"I know you're tired,
but come. This is the way."

ᨘ

Are you jealous of the ocean's generosity?
Why would you refuse to give
this joy to anyone?

Fish don't hold the sacred liquid in cups!
They swim the huge fluid freedom.

11   Union:
Gnats Inside the Wind

ON UNION

There is a great feminine wisdom in these poems, a jemal *quality as opposed to* jelal. *Many of the images of what it's like to be in union have this tone to them. A baby at the mother's breast. A river moving inside the personal fish, taking it to the ocean. Gnats lost in the wind. A dead donkey that has completely melded with a salt flat. The archery champion who lets the arrow fall where he stands. These are not heroic questing images.*

   What is it to praise? Be particles.

   During a night of tornadic wind and lightning-everywhere weather in north Georgia, a friend murmured, "Where do hummingbirds go in this?" The next morning the hummingbirds, the same ones, were back fussing at the feeder. They know a hiding trick the gnats don't. I think sometimes that poems can be places to hide, opisthodamal robe closets simulating the experiences they celebrate.

   What is the soul? Consciousness.

GNATS INSIDE THE WIND

Some gnats come from the grass to speak with Solomon.

"O Solomon, you are the champion of the oppressed.
You give justice to the little guys, and they don't get
any littler than us! We are tiny metaphors
for frailty. Can you defend us?"

"Who has mistreated you?"

"Our complaint is against the wind."

"Well," says Solomon, "you have pretty voices,
you gnats, but remember, a judge cannot listen
to just one side. I must hear both litigants."

"Of course," agree the gnats.

"Summon the East Wind!" calls out Solomon,
and the wind arrives almost immediately.

What happened to the gnat plaintiffs? Gone.

Such is the way of every seeker who comes to complain
at the High Court. When the presence of God arrives,
where are the seekers? First there's dying,
then union, like gnats inside the wind.

MEADOWSOUNDS

We've come again to that knee of seacoast
no ocean can reach.

Tie together all human intellects.
They won't stretch to here.

The sky bares its neck so beautifully,
but gets no kiss. Only a taste.

This is the food that everyone wants,
wandering the wilderness, "Please give us
your manna and quail."

We're here again with the beloved.
This air, a shout. These meadowsounds,
an astonishing myth.

We've come into the presence of the one
who was never apart from us.

When the waterbag is filling, you know
the water carrier's here!

The bag leans lovingly against your shoulder.
"Without you I have no knowledge,
no way to touch anyone."

When someone chews sugarcane,
he's wanting this sweetness.

Inside this globe the soul roars like thunder.
And now silence, my strict tutor.

I won't try to talk about Shams.
Language cannot touch that presence.

AYAZ AND THE KING'S PEARL

One day the king assembled his courtiers.
He handed the minister a glowing pearl.
"What would you say this is worth?"

                              "More gold
than a hundred donkeys could carry."

                              "Break it!"
"Sir, how could I waste your resources
like that?" The king presented him
with a robe of honor for his answer
and took back the pearl. He talked awhile
to the assembly on various topics.

                    Then he put the pearl

in the chamberlain's hand. "What would it sell for?"
"Half a kingdom, God preserve it!"

                              "Break it!"
"My hand could not move to do such a thing."
The king rewarded him with a robe of honor
and an increase in his salary, and so it went
with each of the fifty or sixty courtiers.

One by one, they imitated the minister
and the chamberlain and received new wealth.

Then the pearl was given to Ayaz.

"Can you say how splendid this is?"
"It's more than I can say."

                    "Then break it,

this second, into tiny pieces."

Ayaz had had a dream
about this, and he'd hidden two stones in his sleeve.
He crushed the pearl to powder between them.

As Joseph at the bottom of the well listened
to the end of his story, so such listeners
understand success and un-success as one thing.

Don't worry about forms.
If someone wants your horse,
let him have it. Horses are for
hurrying ahead of the others.

The court assembly screamed at the recklessness
of Ayaz, "How could you do that?"

"What the king says is worth more than any pearl.
I honor the king, not some colored stone."

The princes immediately fell on their knees
and put their foreheads on the ground.

Their sighs went up like a smoke cloud
asking forgiveness. The king gestured
to his executioner as though to say,
"Take out this trash."

Ayaz sprang forward.
"Your mercy makes them bow like this.
Give them their lives! Let them keep hoping
for union with you. They see their forgetfulness
now, as the drunken man did when he said,
'I didn't know what I was doing,' and then
someone pointed out, 'But you invited
that forgetfulness into you. You drank it.
There was a choice!'

They know deeply now how imitation
lulled them to sleep. Don't separate yourself
from them. Look at all their heads against the floor.

Raise their faces into yours. Let them wash
in your cool washing place."

Ayaz and his speech always get to this point
and then the pen breaks. How can a saucer
contain the ocean? The drunks break their cups,
but you poured that wine!

Ayaz said, "You picked me
to crush the pearl. Don't punish the others
for my drunken obedience!
Punish them when I'm sober,
because I'll never be sober again.

Whoever bows down like they are bowing down
will not rise up in his old self again.

Like a gnat in your buttermilk,
they've become your buttermilk.

The mountains are trembling. Their map and compass
are the lines in your palm."

Husam,
I need a hundred mouths to say this,
but I only have this one!

A hundred thousand impressions from the spirit
are wanting to come through here.

I feel stunned
in this abundance, crushed and dead.

PUT THIS DESIGN IN YOUR CARPET

Spiritual experience is a modest woman
who looks lovingly at only one man.

It's a great river where ducks
live happily, and crows drown.

The visible bowl of form contains food
that is both nourishing and a source of heartburn.

There is an unseen presence we honor
that gives the gifts.

You're water. We're the millstone.
You're wind. We're dust blown up into shapes.
You're spirit. We're the opening and closing
of our hands. You're the clarity.
We're this language that tries to say it.
You're joy. We're all the different kinds of laughing.

Any movement or sound is a profession of faith,
as the millstone grinding is explaining how it believes
in the river! No metaphor can say this,
but I can't stop pointing
to the beauty.

Every moment and place says,
"Put this design in your carpet!"

Like the shepherd in Book II,
who wanted to pick the lice off God's robe,
and stitch up God's shoes, I want to be
in such a passionate adoration
that my tent gets pitched against the sky!

Let the beloved come
and sit like a guard dog
in front of the tent.

When the ocean surges,
don't let me just hear it.
Let it splash inside my chest!

HALLAJ

Hallaj said what he said and went to the origin
through the hole in the scaffold.

I cut a cap's worth of cloth from his robe,
and it swamped over me from head to foot.

Years ago, I broke a bunch of roses
from the top of his wall. A thorn from that
is still in my palm, working deeper.

From Hallaj, I learned to hunt lions,
but I became something hungrier than a lion.

I was a frisky colt. He broke me
with a quiet hand on the side of my head.

A person comes to him naked. It's cold.
There's a fur coat floating in the river.

"Jump in and get it," he says.
You dive in. You reach for the coat.
It reaches for you.

It's a live bear that has fallen in upstream,
drifting with the current.

"How long does it take!" Hallaj yells from the bank.
"Don't wait," you answer. "This coat
has decided to wear me home!"

A little part of a story, a hint.
Do you need long sermons on Hallaj!

WE THREE

My love wanders the rooms, melodious,
flute notes, plucked wires,
full of a wine the Magi drank
on the way to Bethlehem.

We are three. The moon comes
from its quiet corner, puts a pitcher of water
down in the center. The circle
of surface flames.

One of us kneels to kiss the threshold.

One drinks, with wine-flames playing over his face.

One watches the gathering,
and says to any cold onlookers,

This dance is the joy of existence.

I am filled with you.
Skin, blood, bone, brain, and soul.
There's no room for lack of trust, or trust.
Nothing in this existence but that existence.

12 ~ The Sheikh:
I Have Such a Teacher

ON THE SHEIKH

The existence of the beloved is not provable, nor is it fantasy. The Friend, as Rumi usually calls this presence within and infinitely beyond the senses, is elusive and nearer than the big vein on your neck; you need a mirror to see it. The sheikh is a mirror, a reminder of that presence, and a cook. The understanding that comes through a sheikh gives nourishment and transforming energy to many. Rumi's image of a disciple is a chickpea that sprouts and enjoys the rainy garden of sexual pleasure. It matures to its hardened form, then gets picked and thrown in the cooking pot. The cook's tending is careful and constant and, in Rumi's case, garrulous. Gradually the disciple softens and takes on flavors the cook adds. Eventually he or she becomes tasty enough to be appealing to those who in the sufi tradition are called the True Human Beings. So the chickpea moves from garden to cooking pot to a taste for the cook, finally to become sustenance for a mysterious community.

CHICKPEA TO COOK

A chickpea leaps almost over the rim of the pot
where it's being boiled.

"Why are you doing this to me?"

The cook knocks him down with the ladle.

"Don't you try to jump out.
You think I'm torturing you.
I'm giving you flavor,

so you can mix with spices and rice
and be the lovely vitality of a human being."

Remember when you drank rain in the garden.
That was for this."

Grace first. Sexual pleasure,
then a boiling new life begins,
and the Friend has something good to eat.

Eventually the chickpea
will say to the cook,

     "Boil me some more.
Hit me with the skimming spoon.
I can't do this by myself.

I'm like an elephant that dreams of gardens
back in Hindustan and doesn't pay attention
to his driver. You're my cook, my driver,
my way into existence. I love your cooking."

The cook says,

     "I was once like you,
fresh from the ground. Then I boiled in time,
and boiled in the body, two fierce boilings.

My animal soul grew powerful.
I controlled it with practices,
and boiled some more, and boiled
once beyond that,

     and became your teacher."

I HAVE SUCH A TEACHER

Last night my teacher taught me the lesson of poverty,
having nothing and wanting nothing.

I am a naked man standing inside a mine of rubies,
clothed in red silk.
I absorb the shining and now I see the ocean,
billions of simultaneous motions

moving in me.
A circle of lovely, quiet people
becomes the ring on my finger.

Then the wind and thunder of rain on the way.
I have such a teacher.

SUBLIME GENEROSITY

I was dead, then alive.
Weeping, then laughing.

The power of love came into me,
and I became fierce like a lion,
then tender like the evening star.

He said, "You're not mad enough.
You don't belong in this house."

I went wild and had to be tied up.
He said, "Still not wild enough
to stay with us!"

I broke through another layer
into joyfulness.

He said, "It's not enough."
I died.

He said, "You're a clever little man,
full of fantasy and doubting."

I plucked out my feathers and became a fool.
He said, "Now you're the candle
for this assembly."

But I'm no candle. Look!
I'm scattered smoke.

He said, "You are the sheikh, the guide."
But I'm not a teacher. I have no power.

He said, "You already have wings.
I cannot give you wings."

But I wanted *his* wings.
I felt like some flightless chicken.

Then new events said to me,
"Don't move. A sublime generosity is
coming toward you."

And old love said, "Stay with me."

I said, "I will."

You are the fountain of the sun's light.
I am a willow shadow on the ground.
You make my raggedness silky.

The soul at dawn is like darkened water
that slowly begins to say *Thank you, thank you.*

Then at sunset, again, Venus gradually
changes into the moon and then the whole nightsky.

This comes of smiling back
at your smile.

The chess master says nothing,
other than moving the silent chess piece.

That I am part of the ploys
of this game makes me
amazingly happy.

LIKE THIS

If anyone asks you
how the perfect satisfaction
of all our sexual wanting
will look, lift your face
and say,
          Like this.

When someone mentions the gracefulness
of the nightsky, climb up on the roof
and dance and say,
                    Like this?

If anyone wants to know what "spirit" is,
or what "God's fragrance" means,
lean your head toward him or her.
Keep your face there close.

Like this.

When someone quotes the old poetic image
about clouds gradually uncovering the moon,
slowly loosen knot by knot the strings
of your robe.

Like this?

If anyone wonders how Jesus raised the dead,
don't try to explain the miracle.
Kiss me on the lips.

Like this. Like this.

When someone asks what it means
to "die for love," point

here.

If someone asks how tall I am, frown
and measure with your fingers the space
between the creases on your forehead.

This tall.

The soul sometimes leaves the body, then returns.
When someone doesn't believe that,
walk back into my house.

Like this.

When lovers moan,
they're telling our story.

Like this.

I am a sky where spirits live.
Stare into this deepening blue,
while the breeze says a secret.

Like this.

When someone asks what there is to do,
light the candle in his hand.

Like this.

How did Joseph's scent come to Jacob?

     Huuuuu.

How did Jacob's sight return?

     Huuuu.

A little wind cleans the eyes.

     Like this.

When Shams comes back from Tabriz,
he'll put just his head around the edge
of the door to surprise us.

     Like this.

A BOWL

Imagine the time the particle you are
returns where it came from!

The family darling comes home. Wine,
without being contained in cups,
is handed around.

A red glint appears in a granite outcrop,
and suddenly the whole cliff turns to ruby.

At dawn I walked along with a monk
on his way to the monastery.

     "We do the same work,"
I told him. "We suffer the same."

He gave me a bowl.
And I saw:
 the soul has *this* shape.

    Shams,
you that teach us and actual sunlight,

      help me now,

being in the middle of being partly in my self,
and partly outside.

WAX

When I see you and how you are,
I close my eyes to the other.
For your Solomon's seal I become wax
throughout my body. I wait to be light.
I give up opinions on all matters.
I become the reed flute for your breath.

You were inside my hand.
I kept reaching around for something.
I was inside your hand, but I kept asking questions
of those who know very little.

I must have been incredibly simple or drunk or insane
to sneak into my own house and steal money,
to climb over the fence and take my own vegetables.
But no more. I've gotten free of that ignorant fist
that was pinching and twisting my secret self.

The universe and the light of the stars come through me.
I am the crescent moon put up
over the gate to the festival.

NO ROOM FOR FORM

On the night when you cross the street
from your shop and your house
to the cemetery,

you'll hear me hailing you from inside
the open grave, and you'll realize
how we've always been together.

I am the clear consciousness-core
of your being, the same in
ecstasy as in self-hating fatigue.

That night, when you escape the fear of snakebite
and all irritation with the ants, you'll hear
my familiar voice, see the candle being lit,

smell the incense, the surprise meal fixed
by the lover inside all your other lovers.

This heart-tumult is my signal
to you igniting in the tomb.

So don't fuss with the shroud
and the graveyard road dust.

Those get ripped open and washed away
in the music of our finally meeting.

And don't look for me in a human shape.
I am inside your looking. No room
for form with love this strong.

Beat the drum and let the poets speak.
This is a day of purification for those who
are already mature and initiated into what love is.

No need to wait until we die!
There's more to want here than money
and being famous and bites of roasted meat.

Now, what shall we call this new sort of gazing-house
that has opened in our town where people sit
quietly and pour out their glancing
like light, like answering?

CHILDHOOD FRIENDS

You may have heard, it's the custom for kings
to let warriors stand on the left, the side of the heart,
and courage. On the right they put the chancellor,
and various secretaries, because the practice
of bookkeeping and writing usually belongs
to the right hand. In the center,

                              the sufis,

because in meditation they become mirrors.
The king can look at their faces
and see his original state.

Give the beautiful ones mirrors,
and let them fall in love with themselves.

That way they polish their souls
and kindle remembering in others.

A close childhood friend once came to visit Joseph.
They had shared the secrets that children tell each other
when they're lying on their pillows at night
before they go to sleep. These two
were completely truthful
with each other.

The friend asked, "What was it like when you realized
your brothers were jealous and what they planned to do?"

"I felt like a lion with a chain around its neck.
Not degraded by the chain, and not complaining,
but just waiting for my power to be recognized."

"How about down in the well, and in prison?
How was it then?"
                    "Like the moon when it's getting
smaller, yet knowing the fullness to come.
Like a seed pearl ground in the mortar for medicine,
that knows it will now be the light in a human eye.

Like a wheat grain that breaks open in the ground,
then grows, then gets harvested, then crushed in the mill
for flour, then baked, then crushed again between teeth
to become a person's deepest understanding.
Lost in love, like the songs the planters sing
the night after they sow the seed."
                    There is no end
to any of this.
                    Back to something else the good man
and Joseph talked about.
                    "Ah my friend, what have you
brought me? You know a traveler should not arrive
empty-handed at the door of a friend like me.
That's going to the grinding stone without your wheat.

God will ask at the resurrection, 'Did you bring Me
a present? Did you forget? Did you think
you wouldn't see me?'"
                              Joseph kept teasing,
"Let's have it. I want my gift!"

The guest began, "You can't imagine how I've looked
for something for you. Nothing seemed appropriate.
You don't take gold down into a goldmine,
or a drop of water to the Sea of Oman!
Everything I thought of was like bringing cumin seed
to Kirmanshah where cumin comes from.

You have all seeds in your barn. You even have my love
and my soul, so I can't even bring those.

I've brought you a mirror. Look at yourself,
and remember me."

                              He took the mirror out from his robe
where he was hiding it.
                              What is the mirror of being?
Non-being. Always bring a mirror of non-existence
as a gift. Any other present is foolish.

Let the poor man look deep into generosity.
Let bread see a hungry man.
Let kindling behold a spark from the flint.

An empty mirror and your worst destructive habits,
when they are held up to each other,
that's when the real making begins.
That's what art and crafting are.

A tailor needs a torn garment to practice his expertise.
The trunks of trees must be cut and cut again
so they can be used for fine carpentry.

Your doctor must have a broken leg to doctor.
Your defects are the ways that glory gets manifested.
Whoever sees clearly what's diseased in himself
begins to gallop on the way.

There is nothing worse
than thinking you are well enough.
More than anything, self-complacency
blocks the workmanship.

Put your vileness up to a mirror and weep.
Get that self-satisfaction flowing out of you!
Satan thought, "I am better than Adam,"
and that *better than* is still strongly in us.

Your stream water may look clean,
but there's unstirred matter on the bottom.
Your sheikh can dig a side channel
that will drain that waste off.

Trust your wound to a teacher's surgery.
Flies collect on a wound. They cover it,
those flies of your self-protecting feelings,
your love for what you think is yours.

Let a teacher wave away the flies
and put a plaster on the wound.

Don't turn your head. Keep looking
at the bandaged place. That's where
the light enters you.
                    And don't believe for a moment
that you're healing yourself.

THE MOUSE AND THE CAMEL

A mouse caught hold of a camel's lead rope
in his two forelegs and walked off with it,
imitating the camel drivers.
                    The camel went along,
letting the mouse feel heroic.
                    "Enjoy yourself,"
he thought. "I have something to teach you, presently."

They came to the edge of a great river.
The mouse was dumbfounded.

"What are you waiting for?
Step forward into the river. You are my leader.
Don't stop here."
"I'm afraid of being drowned."

The camel walked into the water. "It's only
just above the knee."
"*Your* knee! Your knee
is a hundred times over my head!"
"Well, maybe you shouldn't
be leading a camel. Stay with those like yourself.
A mouse has nothing really to say to a camel."

"Would you help me get across?"

"Get up on my hump. I am made to take hundreds like you
    across."

You are not a prophet, but go humbly on the way of the prophets,

and you can arrive where they are. Don't try to steer the boat.
Don't open a shop by yourself. Listen. Keep silent.
You are not God's mouthpiece. Try to be an ear,
and if you do speak, ask for explanations.

The source of your arrogance and anger is your lust
and the rootedness of that is in your habits.

Someone who makes a habit of eating clay
gets mad when you try to keep him from it.
Being a leader can also be a poisonous habit,
so that when someone questions your authority,
you think, "He's trying to take over."
You may respond courteously, but inside you rage.

Always check your inner state
with the lord of your heart.
Copper doesn't know it's copper,
until it's changed to gold.

Your loving doesn't know its majesty,
until it knows its helplessness.

🔊

These gifts from the Friend, a robe
of skin and veins, a teacher within,
wear them and become a school,
with a greater sheikh nearby.

THE LAME GOAT

You've seen a herd of goats
going down to the water.

The lame and dreamy goat
brings up the rear.

There are worried faces about that one,
but now they're laughing,

because look, as they return,
that goat is leading!

There are many different kinds of knowing.
The lame goat's kind is a branch
that traces back to the roots of presence.

Learn from the lame goat,
and lead the herd home.

13 ☙ Recognizing Elegance:
Your Reasonable Father

ON ELEGANCE

The sudden opening of one's eyes to the elaborate, extravagant beauty around us. Watching Madagascan meerkats on the Discovery channel. The gorgeous dirt road down to the river. Three hundred million galaxies. The gold around a frog's eye. The intricacy of the present moment, all the wealth we need. Rumi feels this abundance, and his gratitude for it pours out the waterfall of his work.

It may be that the clarity Rumi calls "reason" is a brilliant lawfulness that ecologists and astronomers examine as the coherence in any system, and that the mystic and the scientist both attend the same layered intelligence: the grand and precise artistry of existence.

FATHER REASON

The universe is a form of divine law,
your reasonable father.

When you feel ungrateful to him,
the shapes of the world seem mean and ugly.

Make peace with that father, the elegant patterning,
and every experience will fill with immediacy.

Because I love this, I am never bored.
Beauty constantly wells up, a noise of springwater
in my ear and in my inner being.

Tree limbs rise and fall like the ecstatic arms
of those who have submitted to the mystical life.

Leaf sounds talk together like poets
making fresh metaphors. The green felt cover slips,
and we get a flash of the mirror underneath.

Think how it will be when the whole thing
is pulled away! I tell only one one-thousandth
of what I see, because there's so much doubt everywhere.

The conventional opinion of this poetry is,
it shows great optimism for the future.

But Father Reason says,
No need to announce the future!
This now is it. *This.* Your deepest need and desire
is satisfied by the *moment's* energy
here in your hand.

꒰

A craftsman pulled a reed from the reedbed,
cut holes in it, and called it a human being.

Since then, it's been wailing a tender agony
of parting, never mentioning the skill
that gave it life as a flute.

꒰

Humble living does not diminish. It fills.
Going back to a simpler self gives wisdom.

When a man makes up a story for his child,
he becomes a father and a child
together, listening.

꒰

You've heard about the qualities of Bilal.
Now hear about the thinness of Hilal,
which is more advanced than Bilal.

He denied his *nafs* more than some of you
who move backward, from being an illumined globe
toward becoming again an opaque stone.

Remember the story of the young guest
who came before a certain king. "And how old are you,
my lad? Tell the truth now. Say it out."

"Eighteen, well seventeen.   Sixteen.
Actually, uh, fifteen."

"Keep going! You'll end up
in your mother's womb."

Or the man who went to borrow a horse.
"Take the gray."

                    "No, not that one."
"Why?"
                "It goes in reverse. It backs up."

"Then turn its tail toward your home."

The beast you ride is your various appetites.
Change your wantings. When you prune
weak branches, the remaining fruit
get tastier. Lust can be redirected,
so that even when it takes you backward,
it goes toward shelter.

A strong intention can make "two oceans wide"
be the size of a blanket, or "seven hundred years"
the time it takes to walk to someone you love.

True seekers keep riding straight through,
whereas big, lazy, self-worshiping geese
unload their pack animals in a farmyard
and say, "This is far enough."

Do you know the story of the travelers
who came to a village in early Spring?
There's an abandoned house with an open door.

"Why don't we wait for this cold spell to pass,
this *old woman's chill,* they call it.
Let's put our baggage in here and rest."

A deep voice from inside, "No. Unload outside,
then enter. This is a meeting hall
of great dignity!"

There are such secret sanctuaries.

Although he worked in a stable as a groom,
Hilal was an enlightened master.

His employer did not understand Hilal's state.
He knew up and down and north-south-east-west,
the evidence of the senses, but nothing else.

The color of the ground is in front of us,
but prophetic light is hidden.

One person sees a minaret, but not the bird
perched there. A second person sees the bird,
but not the hair it carries. A third
sees minaret, bird, and hair.

Until you can see the thread of the hair,
the knot of awareness will not be loosened.

The body is the minaret. Obedience,
the bird. Or three hundred birds, or two,
however you want it. The second person
sees the bird, and only the bird.

The hair is the secret
that belongs to the bird.

No nest built with such material
will go unused. A song-thread flows
continuously out of the bird.

Try to see this bird on its clay tower,
and also the hair floating in its beak.

Hilal becomes ill. Nine days he lies sick
in the stable. No one notices,
except the prophet Muhammad, peace
and blessing be upon him.
He comes to visit.

Hilal's employer is ecstatic.
With elaborate ceremony he emerges
from his upstairs room and kisses the ground
in front of the Prophet. "In God's name,
please honor this house."

"I'm not here to visit you."

"Who then?"

"There is a new-moon new-man planted near here,
spending the lightness of his humility
like blossoms on the ground.
Where is Hilal?"

"I haven't seen him for days.
He must be out with the mules and the horses."

Muhammad runs to the stable. It's dark,
and the stench of manure is strong,
but all that vanishes when friendship enters.

Miracles don't cause faith, but rather
the scent of kindredness that unites people.

Miracles overwhelm unbelief.
Faith grows from friendship.

With the familiar fragrance, Hilal wakes up.
How could such a thing be in a stable?

Through the legs of the horses he sees
the robes of Muhammad! He comes crawling out
from the dark corner and lays his cheek

on Muhammad's feet. Muhammad puts his cheek
on Hilal's and kisses his head and face.

"How hidden can one be!
Are you better? How are you?"

HOW!

A man sits and eats damp clay for moisture.
How is it with him when a flood of fresh
prophetic rainwater suddenly rides him along?

How is it when a blind, filthy dog wakes up,
and finds that he's a lion, and not
a lion such as could be killed,
but a spirit-lion who shatters sword
and javelin with just his presence?

How would that feel? A man crawls for years
on his stomach with his eyes closed.
Then one moment he opens his eyes,
and he's in a garden. It's Spring.

How is it to be free of HOW,
loose in howlessness?

Howlers sit waiting around your table.
Throw them a bone!

This suggestion: wash before going to the watertank.
The waters there have grace enough to clean
and give you peace, but wash yourself
of *hows* before you go.

Wash off all wonderings-why
and workings-out-however.
Don't take those with you
to the big watertank.

Husam! Bats don't bother Husamuddin.
He's an expert on sunlight!

He's written about the new moon, Hilal.
Now he'll write about the full moon, the sheikh.
New moon and full moon are the same.

A new moon teaches gradualness
and deliberation and how one gives birth
to oneself slowly. Patience with small details
makes perfect a large work, like the universe.

What nine months of attention does for an embryo
forty early mornings will do
for your gradually growing wholeness.

BODY INTELLIGENCE

Your intelligence is always with you,
overseeing your body, even though
you may not be aware of its work.

If you start doing something against
your health, your intelligence
will eventually scold you.

If it hadn't been so lovingly close by,
and so constantly monitoring,
how could it rebuke?

You and your intelligence
are like the beauty and the precision
of an astrolabe.

Together, you calculate how near
existence is to the sun!

Your intelligence is marvelously intimate.
It's not in front of you or behind,
or to the left or the right.

Now try, my friend, to describe how near
is the creator of your intellect!

Intellectual searching will not find
the way to that king!

The movement of your finger
is not separate from your finger.

You go to sleep, or you die,
and there's no intelligent motion.

Then you wake,
and your fingers
fill with meanings.

Now consider the jewel-lights
in your eyes. How do *they* work?

This visible universe has many weathers
and variations.
                But uncle, O uncle,
the universe of the creation-word,
the divine command to *Be*, that universe
of qualities is beyond any pointing to.

More intelligent than intellect,
and more spiritual than spirit.

No being is unconnected
to that reality, and that connection
cannot be said. *There*, there's
no separation and no return.

There are guides who can show you the way.
Use them. But they will not satisfy your longing.

Keep wanting that connection
with all your pulsing energy.

The throbbing vein
will take you further
than any thinking.

Muhammad said, "Don't theorize
about essence!" All speculations
are just more layers of covering.
Human beings love coverings!

They think the designs on the curtains
are what's being concealed.

Observe the wonders as they occur around you.
Don't claim them. Feel the artistry
moving through, and be silent.

Or say, "I cannot praise You
as You should be praised.

Such words are infinitely
beyond my understanding."

THE SEED MARKET

Can you find another market like this?

Where,
with your one rose
you can buy hundreds of rose gardens?

Where,
for one seed
you get a whole wilderness?

For one weak breath,
the divine wind?

You've been fearful
of being absorbed in the ground,
or drawn up by the air.

Now, your waterbead lets go
and drops into the ocean,
where it came from.

It no longer has the form it had,
but it's still water.
The essence is the same.

This giving up is not a repenting.
It's a deep honoring of yourself.

When the ocean comes to you as a lover,
marry, at once, quickly,
for God's sake!

Don't postpone it!
Existence has no better gift.

No amount of searching
will find this.

A perfect falcon, for no reason,
has landed on your shoulder,
and become yours.

14 ❧ The Howling Necessity:
Cry Out in Your Weakness

ON HOWLING

My sufi teacher, Bawa Muhaiyaddeen, when he saw me, and knowing my name was Barks, would go into a wolf howl for a joke and a teaching. He mirrored some need to howl that he saw there walking in. He himself would often break into spontaneous praise songs while sitting on his bed. Crying out loud for help is Rumi's point. With that vulnerable breaking open in the psyche, the milk of grace starts to flow.

LOVE DOGS

One night a man was crying,
> *Allah! Allah!*
His lips grew sweet with the praising,
until a cynic said,
> "So! I have heard you
calling out, but have you ever
gotten any response?"

The man had no answer to that.
He quit praying and fell into a confused sleep.

He dreamed he saw Khidr, the guide of souls,
in a thick, green foliage.
> "Why did you stop praising?"
"Because I've never heard anything back."
> "This longing
you express *is* the return message."

The grief you cry out from
draws you toward union.

Your pure sadness
that wants help
is the secret cup.

Listen to the moan of a dog for its master.
That whining is the connection.

There are love dogs
no one knows the names of.

Give your life
to be one of them.

CRY OUT IN YOUR WEAKNESS

A dragon was pulling a bear into its terrible mouth.

A courageous man went and rescued the bear.
There are such helpers in the world, who rush to save
anyone who cries out. Like Mercy itself,
they run toward the screaming.

And they can't be bought off.
If you were to ask one of those, "Why did you come
so quickly?" he or she would say, "Because I heard
your helplessness."
                        Where lowland is,
that's where water goes. All medicine wants
is pain to cure.
                        And don't just ask for one mercy.
Let them flood in. Let the sky open under your feet.
Take the cotton out of your ears, the cotton
of consolations, so you can hear the sphere-music.
Push the hair out of your eyes.
Blow the phlegm from your nose,
and from your brain.

Let the wind breeze through.
Leave no residue in yourself from that bilious fever.
Take the cure for impotence,

that your manhood may shoot forth,
and a hundred new beings come of your coming.

Tear the binding from around the foot
of your soul, and let it race around the track
in front of the crowd. Loosen the knot of greed
so tight on your neck. Accept your new good luck.

Give your weakness
to one who helps.

Crying out loud and weeping are great resources.
A nursing mother, all she does
is wait to hear her child.

Just a little beginning-whimper,
and she's there.

God created the child, that is, your wanting,
so that it might cry out, so that milk might come.

Cry out! Don't be stolid and silent
with your pain. Lament! And let the milk
of loving flow into you.

The hard rain and wind
are ways the cloud has
to take care of us.

Be patient.
Respond to every call
that excites your spirit.

Ignore those that make you fearful
and sad, that degrade you
back toward disease and death.

THE DEBTOR SHEIKH

Sheikh Ahmad was continually in debt.
He borrowed great sums from the wealthy
and gave it out to the poor dervishes of the world.
He built a sufi monastery by borrowing,

and God was always paying his debts, turning sand
into flour for this generous friend.

The Prophet said that there were always two angels
praying in the market. One said, "Lord,
give the poor wanderer help." The other, "Lord,
give the miser a poison." Especially loud
is the former prayer when the wanderer is a prodigal
like Sheikh Ahmad, the debtor sheikh.

For years, until his death, he scattered seed profusely.
Even very near his death, with the signs of death clear,
he sat surrounded by creditors. The creditors in a circle,
and the great sheikh in the center gently melting
into himself like a candle.

The creditors were so sour-faced with worry
that they could hardly breathe.

"Look at these despairing men," thought the sheikh.
"Do they think God does not have four hundred gold dinars?"
Just at that moment a boy outside called,

                                "Halvah, a sixth
of a dirhem for a piece! Fresh halvah!"

                                   Sheikh Ahmad,
with a nod of his head, directed the famulus
to go and buy the whole tray of halvah.

"Maybe if these creditors eat a little sweetness,
they won't look so bitterly on me."

The servant went to the boy, "How much for the whole lump
of halvah?"

                    "Half a dinar, and some change."

"Don't ask too much from sufis, my son.
Half a dinar is enough."

The boy handed over the tray, and the servant brought it
to the sheikh, who passed it among his creditor guests.
"Please, eat, and be happy."

The tray was quickly emptied, and the boy asked the sheikh
for his half a gold dinar.

"Where would I find such money? These men can tell you
how in debt I am, and besides, I am fast on my way
into non-existence."

                         The boy threw the tray on the floor
and started weeping loud and yelling,

                              "I wish
I had broken my legs before I came in here!

                                        I wish
I'd stayed in the bathhouse today. You gluttonous,
plate-licking sufis, washing your faces like cats!"

A crowd gathered. The boy continued, "O sheikh,
my master will beat me if I come back without anything."

The creditors joined in, "How could you do this?
You've devoured our properties, and now you add this
one last debt before you die.

                         Why?"

The sheikh closes his eyes and does not answer.
The boy weeps until afternoon prayers. The sheikh
withdraws underneath his coverlet,

                                        pleased with everything,
pleased with eternity, pleased with death,

                                        and totally
unconcerned with all the reviling talk around him.

On a bright-moon night, do you think the moon,
cruising through the tenth house, can hear the dogs barking
down here?

                    But the dogs are doing what they're supposed to do.
Water does not lose its purity because of a bit of weed
floating in it.

                    That king drinks wine on the riverbank
until dawn, listening to the water music, not hearing
the frog talk.

                    The money due the boy would have been
just a few pennies from each of his creditors, but the sheikh's
spiritual power prevents that from happening.
No one gives the boy anything.

At afternoon prayers a servant comes with a tray
from Hatim, a friend of Ahmad's, and a man
of great property. A covered tray.

The sheikh uncovers the face of the tray, and on it
there are four hundred gold dinars, and in one corner,
another half a dinar wrapped in a piece of paper.

Immediately the cries of abasement, "O king of sheikhs,
lord of the lords of mystery! Forgive us.
We were bumbling and crazed. We were knocking lamps over.
We were . . . "

            "It's all right. You will not be held
responsible for what you've said or done. The secret here
is that I asked God and the way was shown
that until the boy's weeping, God's merciful generosity
was not loosened.

            Let the boy be like the pupil of your eye.
If you want to wear a robe of spiritual sovereignty,
let your eyes weep with the wanting."

᠅

You that come to birth and bring the mysteries,
your voice-thunder makes us very happy.

Roar, lion of the heart,
and tear me open!

15 ✒ Teaching Stories:
How the Unseen World Works

ON THE UNSEEN

Ibn Khafif Shirazi tells this story: "I heard that there were two great masters in Egypt, so I hurried to reach their presence. When I arrived, I saw two magnificent teachers meditating. I greeted them three times, but they did not answer. I meditated with them for four days. Each day I begged them to talk with me, since I had come such a long way. Finally the younger one opened his eyes. 'Ibn Khafif, life is short. Use the portion that's left to deepen yourself. Don't waste time greeting people!' I asked him to give me some advice. 'Stay in the presence of those who remind you of your lord, who not only speak wisdom, but are that.' Then he went back into meditation." Ibn Khafif was being taught the importance of having his own experience of the unseen, and not to fret so much about the forms of greeting people, hearing wisdom, and about what we should be doing.

There is a South Indian story about soap. Soap is the dirt we buy. We introduce it to the dirt we have, and the two dirts are so glad to see each other they come out and mix! They swim together in the warm pleasurable water and, at just the right moment, the washer lifts the cloth of our true being free of both soap and dirt. Mystical poetry and other practices may function this way, as soap that dances with what disturbs our clarity. Then at some moment they drop away and leave us clean, ready to be worn again.

NASUH

Some time ago there was a man named Nasuh.
He made his living shampooing women in a bathhouse.
He had a face like a woman, but he was not effeminate,
though he disguised his virility, so as to keep his job.

He loved touching the women as he washed their hair.
He stayed sexually alert, at full strength,
all the time, massaging the beautiful women,
especially the Princess and her ladies-in-waiting.

Sometimes he thought of changing jobs,
of doing something
where he wouldn't be so constantly lustful,
but he couldn't quit.

He went to a mystic saint and said,
"Please remember me in a prayer."

That holy man was spiritually free,
and totally opened to God. He knew Nasuh's secret,
but with God's gentleness he didn't speak it.

A gnostic says little, but inside he is full of mysteries,
and crowded with voices. Whoever is served
that cup keeps quiet.

The holy man laughed softly and prayed aloud,
"May God cause you to change your life
in the way you know you should."

The prayer of such a sheikh is different
from other prayers. He has so completely dissolved
his ego, nothinged himself, that what he says
is like God talking to God. How could
such a prayer not be granted?

The means were found to change Nasuh.
While he was pouring water into a basin
for a naked woman, she felt and discovered
that a pearl was missing from her earring.

Quickly, they locked the doors.
They searched the cushions, the towels, the rugs,
and the discarded clothes. Nothing.
                                   Now they search
ears and mouths and every cleft and orifice.

Everyone is made to strip,
and the queen's lady chamberlain

probes one by one
the naked women.
                    Nasuh, meanwhile,
has gone to his private closet, trembling.

"I didn't steal the pearl,
but if they undress and search me,
they'll see how excited I get
with these nude ladies.
                    God, please,
help me!
          I have been cold and lecherous,
but cover my sin this time, PLEASE!
Let me not be exposed for how I've been.
I'll repent!"
                    He weeps and moans and weeps,
for the moment is upon him.
                         "Nasuh!
We have searched everyone but you. Come out!"

At that moment his spirit grows wings, and lifts.
His ego falls like a battered wall.
He unites with God, alive,
but emptied of
Nasuh.

His ship sinks and in its place move the ocean waves.
His body's disgrace, like a falcon's loosened binding,
slips from the falcon's foot.

His stones drink in water.
His field shines like satin with gold threads in it.
Someone dead a hundred years steps out well
and strong and handsome.
                    A broken stick
breaks into bud.

This all happens inside Nasuh,
after the call that gave him such fear.

A long pause.
A long, waiting silence.

Then a shout from one of the women, "Here it is!"
The bathhouse fills with clapping.
Nasuh sees his new life sparkling out before him.

The women come to apologize, "We're so sorry
we didn't trust you. We just knew
that you'd taken that pearl."

They kept talking about how they'd suspected him,
and begging his forgiveness.

Finally he replies,

       "I am much more guilty
than anyone has thought or said. I am the worst person
in the world. What you have said is only a hundredth
of what I've actually done. Don't ask my pardon!

You don't know me. No one knows me.
God has hidden my sneakiness. Satan taught me tricks,
but after a time, those became easy, and I taught Satan
some new variations. God saw what I did, but chose
not to publicly reveal my sin.

And now, I am sewn back into wholeness!
Whatever I've done,

       now was not done.
Whatever obedience I didn't do,

       now I did!
Pure, noble, free, like a cypress,

       like a lily,
is how I suddenly am. I said,

       Oh no!
Help me!

       And that *Oh no!* became a rope
let down in my well. I've climbed out to stand here
in the sun. One moment I was at the bottom
of a dank, fearful narrowness, and the next,

I am not contained by this universe.

If every tip of every hair on me could speak,
I still couldn't say my gratitude.

In the middle of these streets and gardens, I stand and say
and say again, and it's all I say,
I wish everyone
could know what I know."

MOSES AND THE SHEPHERD

Moses heard a shepherd on the road praying,
                                                "God,
where are you? I want to help you, to fix your shoes
and comb your hair. I want to wash your clothes
and pick the lice off. I want to bring you milk
to kiss your little hands and feet when it's time
for you to go to bed. I want to sweep your room
and keep it neat. God, my sheep and goats
are yours. All I can say, remembering you,
is *ayyyy* and *ahhhhhhhhh."*
                              Moses could stand it no longer.
"Who are you talking to?"
                              "The one who made us,
and made the earth and made the sky."
                                        "Don't talk about shoes
and socks with God! And what's this with *your little hands*
and feet? Such blasphemous familiarity sounds like
you're chatting with your uncles.
                              Only something that grows
needs milk. Only someone with feet needs shoes. Not God!
Even if you meant God's human representatives,
as when God said, 'I was sick, and you did not visit me,'
even then this tone would be foolish and irreverent.

Use appropriate terms. *Fatima* is a fine name
for a woman, but if you call a man *Fatima,*
it's an insult. Body-and-birth language
are right for us on this side of the river,
but not for addressing the origin,
                              not for Allah."

The shepherd repented and tore his clothes and sighed
and wandered out into the desert.

A sudden revelation
came then to Moses. God's voice:

You have separated me
from one of my own. Did you come as a Prophet to unite,
or to sever?

I have given each being a separate and unique way
of seeing and knowing and saying that knowledge.

What seems wrong to you is right for him.
What is poison to one is honey to someone else.

Purity and impurity, sloth and diligence in worship,
these mean nothing to me.

I am apart from all that.
Ways of worshiping are not to be ranked as better
or worse than one another.

Hindus do Hindu things.
The Dravidian Muslims in India do what they do.
It's all praise, and it's all right.

It's not me that's glorified in acts of worship.
It's the worshipers! I don't hear the words
they say. I look inside at the humility.

That broken-open lowliness is the reality,
not the language! Forget phraseology.
I want burning, burning.

Be friends
with your burning. Burn up your thinking
and your forms of expression!

Moses,
those who pay attention to ways of behaving
and speaking are one sort.

Lovers who burn
are another.

Don't impose a property tax
on a burned-out village. Don't scold the Lover.
The "wrong" way he talks is better than a hundred

"right" ways of others.

Inside the Kaaba
it doesn't matter which direction you point
your prayer rug!

The ocean diver doesn't need snowshoes!
The love-religion has no code or doctrine.

Only God.

So the ruby has nothing engraved on it!
It doesn't need markings.

God began speaking
deeper mysteries to Moses. Vision and words,
which cannot be recorded here, poured into
and through him. He left himself and came back.
He went to eternity and came back here.
Many times this happened.

It's foolish of me
to try and say this. If I did say it,
it would uproot our human intelligences.
It would shatter all writing pens.

Moses ran after the shepherd.
He followed the bewildered footprints,
in one place moving straight like a castle
across a chessboard. In another, sideways,
like a bishop.

Now surging like a wave cresting,
now sliding down like a fish,

with always his feet
making geomancy symbols in the sand,

recording
his wandering state.

Moses finally caught up
with him.

"I was wrong. God has revealed to me
that there are no rules for worship.

Say whatever
and however your loving tells you to. Your sweet blasphemy
is the truest devotion. Through you a whole world
is freed.

Loosen your tongue and don't worry what comes out.
It's all the light of the spirit."

The shepherd replied,
"Moses, Moses,

I've gone beyond even that.
You applied the whip and my horse shied and jumped
out of itself. The divine nature and my human nature
came together.

Bless your scolding hand and your arm.
I can't say what has happened.

What I'm saying now
is not my real condition. It can't be said."

The shepherd grew quiet.

When you look in a mirror,
you see yourself, not the state of the mirror.
The flute player puts breath into a flute,
and who makes the music? Not the flute.
The flute player!

Whenever you speak praise
or thanksgiving to God, it's always like
this dear shepherd's simplicity.

When you eventually see
through the veils to how things really are,
you will keep saying again
and again,

"This is certainly not like
we thought it was!"

JOY AT SUDDEN DISAPPOINTMENT

Whatever comes, comes from a need,
a sore distress, a hurting want.

Mary's pain made the baby Jesus.
Her womb opened its lips
and spoke the Word.

Every part of you has a secret language.
Your hands and your feet say what you've done.

And every need brings in what's needed.
Pain bears its cure like a child.

Having nothing produces provisions.
Ask a difficult question,
and the marvelous answer appears.

Build a ship, and there'll be water
to float it. The tender-throated
infant cries and milk drips
from the mother's breast.

Be thirsty for the ultimate water,
and then be ready for what will
come pouring from the spring.

A village woman once was walking by Muhammad.
She thought he was just an ordinary illiterate.
She didn't believe that he was a prophet.

She was carrying a two-month-old baby.
As she came near Muhammad, the baby turned
and said, "Peace be with you, Messenger of God."

The mother cried out, surprised and angry,
"What are you saying,
and how can you suddenly talk!"

The child replied, "God taught me first,
and then Gabriel."
                    "Who is this Gabriel?
I don't see anyone."
                    "He is above your head,
Mother. Turn around. He has been telling me
many things."
                    "Do you really see him?"
                                            "Yes.
He is continually delivering me from this
degraded state into sublimity."

Muhammad then asked the child,
"What is your name?"

"Abdul Aziz, the servant of God, but this family
thinks I am concerned with world-energies.
I am as free of that as the truth of your prophecy is."

So the little one spoke, and the mother
took in a fragrance that let her surrender
to that state.
    When God gives this knowing,
inanimate stones, plants, animals, everything,
fills with unfolding significance.

The fish and the birds become protectors.
Remember the incident of Muhammad and the eagle.

It happened that as he was listening
to this inspired baby, he heard a voice
calling him to prayer. He asked for water
to perform ablutions. He washed his hands
and feet, and just as he reached for his boot,

an eagle snatched it away! The boot turned upsidedown
as it lifted, and a poisonous snake dropped out.

The eagle circled and brought the boot back,
saying, "My helpless reverence for you
made this necessary. Anyone who acts
this presumptuously for a legalistic reason
should be punished!"
                    Muhammad thanked the eagle,
and said, "What I thought was rudeness
was really love. You took away my grief,
and I was grieved! God has shown me everything,
but at that moment I was preoccupied within myself."
The eagle,
            "But chosen one, any clarity I have
comes from you!"
                    This spreading radiance
of a True Human Being has great importance.

Look carefully around you and recognize
the luminosity of souls. Sit beside those
who draw you to that.

      Learn from this eagle story
that when misfortune comes, you must quickly praise.

Others may be saying, *Oh no,* but you
will be opening out like a rose
losing itself petal by petal.

Someone once asked a great sheikh
what sufism was.

     "The feeling of joy
when sudden disappointment comes."

The eagle carries off Muhammad's boot
and saves him from snakebite.

Don't grieve for what doesn't come.
Some things that don't happen
keep disasters from happening.

      ❦

If the beloved is everywhere,
the lover is a veil,

but when living itself becomes
the Friend, lovers disappear.

      ❦

STORY WATER

 A story is like water
 that you heat for your bath.

 It takes messages between the fire
 and your skin. It lets them meet,
 and it cleans you!

Very few can sit down
in the middle of the fire itself
like a salamander or Abraham.
We need intermediaries.

A feeling of fullness comes,
but usually it takes some bread
to bring it.

Beauty surrounds us,
but usually we need to be walking
in a garden to know it.

The body itself is a screen
to shield and partially reveal
the light that's blazing
inside your presence.

Water, stories, the body,
all the things we do, are mediums
that hide and show what's hidden.

Study them,
and enjoy this being washed
with a secret we sometimes know,
and then not.

16 ᴈ Rough Metaphors:
More Teaching Stories

ON ROUGHNESS

Some of Rumi's metaphors are rough, raw, and unacceptable to re-
fined tastes. When Reynold Nicholson translated the Mathnawi *into*
English in the 1920s, he chose to render some passages into Latin,
supposing that anyone who knew enough Latin to read them would
be properly shielded from taint. Rumi uses anything human beings
do, no matter how scandalous or cruel or silly, as a lens to examine
soul growth. A gourd crafted to serve as a flange, allowing a donkey's
penis to enter a woman's vagina just to the point of her pleasure but
not far enough to harm her, becomes a metaphor for a device a sheikh
might use to put limits on a disciple. After another graphic, outra-
geously elaborated comparison of breadmaking with lovemaking,
he concludes, "Remember. The way you make love is the way God
will be with you." For Rumi, the bread of every experience offers
nourishment.

ROUGH METAPHORS

Someone said, "there is no dervish, or if there is a dervish,
   that dervish is not there."

Look at a candle flame in bright noon sunlight.
   If you put cotton next to it, the cotton will burn,
      but its light has become completely mixed
         with the sun.

That candlelight you can't find   is what's left of a dervish.

If you sprinkle one ounce of vinegar over
        two hundred tons of sugar,
                no one will ever taste the vinegar.

A deer faints in the paws of a lion. The deer becomes
        another glazed expression on the face of the lion.

These are rough metaphors for what happens to the lover.

There's no one more openly irreverent than a lover. He, or she,
        jumps up on the scale opposite eternity
                and claims to balance it.

And no one more secretly reverent.

A grammar lesson: "The lover died."
        "Lover" is subject and agent, but that can't be!
                The "lover" is defunct.

Only grammatically is the dervish-lover a doer.

In reality, with he or she so overcome,
        so dissolved into love,
                all qualities of doingness
                        disappear.

BIRDWINGS

Your grief for what you've lost lifts a mirror
up to where you're bravely working.

Expecting the worst, you look, and instead,
here's the joyful face you've been wanting to see.

Your hand opens and closes and opens and closes.
If it were always a fist or always stretched open,
you would be paralyzed.

Your deepest presence is in every small contracting
                                    and expanding,
the two as beautifully balanced and coordinated
as birdwings.

I COME BEFORE DAWN

Muhammad says,
                    "I come before dawn
to chain you and drag you off."
It's amazing, and funny, that you have to be pulled away
from being tortured, pulled out
into this Spring garden,
                              but that's the way it is.

Almost everyone must be bound and dragged here.
Only a few come on their own.

Children have to be made to go to school at first.
Then some of them begin to like it.
                                    They run to school.
They expand with the learning.
                              Later, they receive money
because of something they've learned at school,
and they get really excited. They stay up all night,
as watchful and alive as thieves!

Remember the rewards you get for being obedient!

There are two types on the path. Those who come
against their will, the blindly religious people, and those
who obey out of love. The former have ulterior motives.
They want the midwife near, because she gives them milk.
The others love the beauty of the nurse.

The former memorize the prooftexts of conformity,
and repeat them. The latter disappear
into whatever draws them to God.

Both are drawn from the source.
Any movings from the mover.
Any love from the beloved.

CHECKMATE

Borrow the beloved's eyes.
Look through them and you'll see the beloved's face

everywhere. No tiredness, no jaded boredom.
"I shall be your eye and your hand and your loving."
Let that happen, and things
you have hated will become helpers.

A certain preacher always prays long and with enthusiasm
for thieves and muggers that attack people
on the street. "Let your mercy, O Lord,
cover their insolence."
He doesn't pray for the good,
but only for the blatantly cruel.
Why is this? his congregation asks.

"Because they have done me such generous favors.
Every time I turn back toward the things they want.
I run into them, they beat me, and leave me nearly dead
in the road, and I understand, again, that what they want
is not what I want. They keep me on the spiritual path.
That's why I honor them and pray for them."

Those that make you return, for whatever reason,
to God's solitude, be grateful to them.
Worry about the others, who give you
delicious comforts that keep you from prayer.
Friends are enemies sometimes,
and enemies friends.

There is an animal called an *ushghur,* a porcupine.
If you hit it with a stick, it extends its quills
and gets bigger. The soul is a porcupine,
made strong by stick-beating.

So a prophet's soul is especially afflicted,
because it has to become so powerful.

A hide is soaked in tanning liquor and becomes leather.
If the tanner did not rub in the acid,
the hide would get foul-smelling and rotten.

The soul is a newly skinned hide, bloody and gross.
Work on it with manual discipline,
and the bitter tanning acid of grief,
and you'll become lovely, and *very* strong.

If you can't do this work yourself, don't worry.
You don't even have to make a decision,
one way or another. The Friend, who knows
a lot more than you do, will bring difficulties,
and grief, and sickness,

                as medicine, as happiness,
as the essence of the moment when you're beaten,
when you hear *Checkmate,* and can finally say,
with Hallaj's voice,

           I trust you to kill me.

AN AWKWARD COMPARISON

This physical world has no two things alike.
Every comparison is awkwardly rough.

You can put a lion next to a man,
but the placing is hazardous to both.

Say the body is like this lamp.
It has to have a wick and oil. Sleep and food.
If it doesn't get those, it will die,
and it's always burning those up, trying to die.

But where is the sun in this comparison?
It rises, and the lamp's light
mixes with the day.

         Oneness,
which is the reality, cannot be understood
with lamp and sun images. The blurring
of a plural into a unity is wrong.

No image can describe
what of our fathers and mothers,
our grandfathers and grandmothers, remains.

Language does not touch the one
who lives in each of us.

TWO KINDS OF INTELLIGENCE

There are two kinds of intelligence: one acquired,
as a child in school memorizes facts and concepts
from books and from what the teacher says,
collecting information from the traditional sciences
as well as from the new sciences.

With such intelligence you rise in the world.
You get ranked ahead or behind others
in regard to your competence in retaining
information. You stroll with this intelligence
in and out of fields of knowledge, getting always more
marks on your preserving tablets.

There is another kind of tablet, one
already completed and preserved inside you.
A spring overflowing its springbox. A freshness
in the center of the chest. This other intelligence
does not turn yellow or stagnate. It's fluid,
and it doesn't move from outside to inside
through the conduits of plumbing-learning.

This second knowing is a fountainhead
from within you, moving out.

TWO WAYS OF RUNNING

A certain man had a jealous wife
and a very, very appealing maidservant.

The wife was careful not to leave them alone,
ever. For six years they were never left
in a room together.
         But then one day
at the public bath the wife suddenly remembered
that she'd left her silver washbasin at home.

"Please, go get the basin," she told her maid.

The girl jumped to the task, because she knew
that she would finally get to be alone
with the master. She ran joyfully.
                                        She flew,
and desire took them both so quickly
that they didn't even latch the door.

With great speed they joined each other.
When bodies blend in copulation,
spirits also merge.

Meanwhile, the wife back at the bathhouse,
washing her hair, "What have I done!
I've set the cotton-wool on fire!
I've put the ram in with the ewe!"

She washed the clay soap off her hair and ran,
fixing her chador about her as she went.

The maid ran for love. The wife ran out of fear
and jealousy. There is a great difference.

The mystic flies moment to moment.
The fearful ascetic drags along month to month.

But also the length of a "day" to a lover
may be fifty thousand years!

You can't understand this with your mind.
You must burst open!

Fear is nothing to a lover, a tiny piece of thread.
Love is a quality of God. Fear is an attribute
of those who think they serve God, but who are actually
preoccupied with penis and vagina.

You have read in the text where *They love him*
blends with *He loves them*.
                                    Those joining loves
are both qualities of God. Fear is not.

What characteristics do God and human beings
have in common? What is the connection between
what lives in time and what lives in eternity?

If I kept talking about love,
a hundred new combinings would happen,
and still I would not say the mystery.

The fearful ascetic runs on foot, along the surface.
Lovers move like lightning and wind.
                      No contest.
Theologians mumble, rumble-dumble,
necessity and free will,
while lover and beloved
                      pull themselves
into each other.

The worried wife reaches the door
and opens it.
               The maid, disheveled, confused, flushed,
unable to speak.
               The husband begins his five-times prayer.

The wife enters this agitated scene.
As though experimenting with clothes,
the husband holds up some flaps and edges.

She sees his testicles and penis so wet, semen
still dribbling out, spurts of jism and vaginal juices
drenching the thighs of the maid.
                    The wife slaps him
on the side of the head,
                "Is this the way
a man prays, with his balls?
                    Does your penis
long for union like this?
                Is that why
her legs are so covered with this stuff?"

These are good questions
she's asking her "ascetic" husband!

People who renounce desires
often turn, suddenly,
into hypocrites!

THE IMPORTANCE OF GOURDCRAFTING

There was a maidservant
who had cleverly trained a donkey
to perform the services of a man.

From a gourd,
she had carved a flanged device
to fit on the donkey's penis,
to keep him from going too far into her.

She had fashioned it just to the point
of her pleasure, and she greatly enjoyed
the arrangement, as often as she could!

She thrived, but the donkey was getting
a little thin and tired looking.

The mistress began to investigate. One day
she peeked through a crack in the door
and saw the animal's marvelous member
and the delight of the girl
stretched under the donkey.

She said nothing. Later, she knocked on the door
and called the maid out on an errand,
a long and complicated errand.
I won't go into details.

The servant knew what was happening, though.
"Ah, my mistress," she thought to herself,
"you should not send away the expert.

When you begin to work without full knowledge,
you risk your life. Your shame keeps you
from asking me about the gourd, but you must
have that to join with this donkey.
There's a trick you don't know!"

But the woman was too fascinated with her idea
to consider any danger. She led the donkey in

and closed the door, thinking, "With no one around
I can shout in my pleasure."

　　　　　　　　　　　　She was dizzy
with anticipation, her vagina glowing
and singing like a nightingale.

She arranged the chair under the donkey,
as she had seen the girl do. She raised her legs
and pulled him into her.

　　　　　　　　　　　　Her fire kindled more,
and the donkey politely pushed as she urged him to,
pushed through and into her intestines,
and, without a word, she died.

The chair fell one way,
and she the other.

The room was smeared with blood.

　　　　　　　　　　　　Reader,
have you ever seen anyone martyred
for a donkey? Remember what the Qur'an
says about the torment of disgracing yourself.

Don't sacrifice your life to your animal-soul!

If you die of what that leads you to do,
you are just like this woman on the floor.
She is an image of immoderation.

Remember her,
and keep your balance.

The maidservant returns and says, "Yes, you saw
my pleasure, but you didn't see the gourd
that put a limit on it. You opened
your shop before a master
taught you the craft."

BREADMAKING

There was a feast. The king
was heartily in his cups.

He saw a learned scholar walking by.
"Bring him in and give him
some of this fine wine."

Servants rushed out and brought the man
to the king's table, but he was not
receptive. "I had rather drink poison!
I have never tasted wine and never will!
Take it away from me!"

He kept on with these loud refusals,
disturbing the atmosphere of the feast.

This is how it sometimes is
at God's table.

Someone who has *heard* about ecstatic love,
but never tasted it, disrupts the banquet.

If there were a secret passage
from his ear to his throat, everything
in him would change. Initiation would occur.

As it is, he's all fire and no light,
all husk and no kernel.

The king gave orders. "Cupbearer,
do what you must!"

This is how your invisible guide acts,
the chess champion across from you
that always wins. He cuffed
the scholar's head and said,

                              "Taste!"

And, "Again!"
              The cup was drained
and the intellectual started singing
and telling ridiculous jokes.

He joined the garden, snapping his fingers
and swaying. Soon, of course,
he had to pee.

He went out, and there, near the latrine,
was a beautiful woman, one of the king's harem.

His mouth hung open. He wanted her!
Right then, he wanted her!
And she was not unwilling.

They fell to, on the ground.
You've seen a baker rolling dough.
He kneads it gently at first,
then more roughly.

He pounds it on the board.
It softly groans under his palms.
Now he spreads it out
and rolls it flat.

Then he bunches it,
and rolls it all the way out again,
thin. Now he adds water,
and mixes it well.

Now salt,
and a little more salt.

Now he shapes it delicately
to its final shape
and slides it into the oven,
which is already hot.

You remember breadmaking!
This is how your desire
tangles with a desired one.

And it's not just a metaphor
for a man and a woman making love.

Warriors in battle do this too.
A great mutual embrace is always happening
between the eternal and what dies,
between essence and accident.

The sport has different rules
in every case, but it's basically
the same, and remember:

the way you make love is the way
God will be with you.

So these two were lost in their sexual trance.
They did not care anymore about feasting
or wine. Their eyes were closed like
perfectly matching calligraphy lines.

The king went looking for the scholar,
and when he saw them there coupled, commented,

"Well, as it is said, 'A good king
must serve his subjects from his own table!'"

There is joy, a winelike freedom
that dissolves the mind and restores
the spirit, and there is manly fortitude
like the king's, a reasonableness
that accepts the bewildered lostness.

But meditate now on steadfastness
and clarity, and let those be the wings
that lift and soar through the celestial spheres.

The Far Mosque

ON SOLOMON

Solomon and Sheba are types for the courtship story going on in all of Rumi's poetry. King Solomon (luminous divine wisdom) sends messengers to coax the Queen of Sheba (the bodily soul) to leave her kingdom and come live with him. She coyly sends envoys back with foolishly inappropriate gifts, and when she herself finally arrives, she does so with the one thing she cannot bear to leave, her filigreed throne (the body). The marriage of spiritual vision with the body finds many metaphors throughout Rumi's art: Jesus riding the lean donkey, the way a river dissolves into the ocean, dawn sunlight filling a ruby, the nightsky contained in a person's eyes. The ecstatic astonishment within Rumi's poetry comes from his firsthand wonder at how the ocean comes to court the drop!

I once had a dream where I was supposed to give a lecture on Rumi and D. H. Lawrence, but I couldn't find the lecture hall. The challenge was to connect Lawrence's dark body-knowledge with Rumi's spiritual enlightenment. I ended up in some anteroom eating hors d'oeuvres. The mind knows when it's been assigned work outside its purview. Rumi's poetry nourishes the part of us that wants a continually unfolding truth, not some confined conclusion. The relationship of soul wisdom and the body, Solomon and Sheba, is a dynamic dance that keeps generating stories.

SHEBA'S GIFTS TO SOLOMON

Queen Sheba loads forty mules with gold bricks
as gifts for Solomon. When her envoy and his party
reach the wide plain leading to Solomon's palace,

they see that the top layer of the entire plain
is pure gold. They travel on gold
for forty days!
            What foolishness to take gold
to Solomon, when the *dirt* of his land
is gold. You who think to offer
your intelligence, reconsider. The mind
is less than road dust.

The embarrassing commonness they bring only
slows them down. They argue. They discuss
turning back, but they continue,
carrying out the orders of their queen.

Solomon laughs when he sees them unloading
gold bars.
            "When have I asked you
for a sop for my soup? I don't want gifts
from you. I want you to be ready
for the gifts I give.

You worship a planet that creates gold.
Worship instead the one who creates the universe.
You worship the sun. The sun is only a cook.
Think of a solar eclipse. What if you get attacked
at midnight? Who will help you then?"

These astronomical matters fade.
Another intimacy happens,

a sun at midnight,
with no east, no night or day.

The clearest intelligences faint,
seeing the solar system flickering,
so tiny in that immense lightness.

Drops fall into a vapor, and the vapor explodes
into a galaxy. Half a ray strikes a patch of darkness.
A new sun appears.
            One slight, alchemical gesture,
and saturnine qualities form inside
the planet Saturn.

The sensuous eye needs sunlight to see.
Use another eye.
                    Vision is luminous.
Sight is igneous, and sun-fire light very dark.

SOLOMON TO SHEBA

Solomon says to the messengers from Sheba,
"I send you back as messengers to her.

Tell her this refusal of her gift
of gold is better than acceptance,

because with it she can learn what *we* value.
She loves her throne, but actually it keeps

her from passing through the doorway
that leads to a true majesty.

Tell her, one surrendering bow is sweeter
than a hundred empires, is itself a kingdom.

Be dizzy and wandering like Ibrahim,
who suddenly left everything.

In a narrow well things look backward
from how they are. Stones and metal objects

seem treasure, as broken pottery does
to children pretending to buy and sell.

Tell her, Joseph sat in such a well,
then reached to take the rope that rose

to a new understanding. The *alchemy*
of a changing life is the only truth."

SHEBA'S HESITATION

Lovers of God, sometimes a door opens,
and a human being becomes a way
for grace to come through.

I see various herbs in the kitchen garden,
each with its own bed, garlic, capers, saffron,
and basil, each watered differently to help it mature.

We keep the delicate ones separate from the turnips,
but there's room for all in this unseen world, so vast
that the Arabian desert gets lost in it like a single hair

in the ocean. Imagine that you are Sheba
trying to decide whether to go to Solomon!
You're haggling about how much to pay

for shoeing a donkey, when you could be seated
with one who is always in union with God,
who carries a beautiful garden inside himself.

You could be moving in a circuit without wing,
nourished without eating, sovereign without a throne.
No longer subject to fortune, you could be *luck* itself,

if you would rise from sleep, leave
the market arguing, and learn that
your own essence *is* your wealth.

SHEBA'S THRONE

When the Queen of Sheba came to Solomon,
she left behind her kingdom and her wealth
the same way lovers leave their reputations.

Her servants meant nothing to her,
less than a rotten onion.

Her palaces and orchards,
so many piles of dung.

She heard the inner meaning of LA! No!
She came to Solomon with nothing, except
her throne! As the writer's pen becomes

a friend, as the tool the workman uses
day after day becomes deeply familiar, so
her filigreed throne was her one attachment.

I would explain more about this phenomenon,
but it would take too long.

It was a large throne and difficult to transport,
because it couldn't be taken apart, being as
cunningly put together as the human body.

Solomon saw that her heart was open to him
and that this throne would soon be repulsive
to her. "Let her bring it," he said. "It will

become a lesson to her like the old shoes
and jacket are to Ayaz. She can look at
that throne and see how far she's come."

In the same way, God keeps the process
of generation constantly before us:

the smooth skin and the semen
and the growing embryo.

When you see a pearl on the bottom,
you reach through the foam and broken sticks
on the surface. When the sun comes up, you forget
about locating the constellation of Scorpio.

When you see the splendor of union,
the attractions of duality seem poignant
and lovely, but much less interesting.

SOLOMON'S CROOKED CROWN

Solomon was busy judging others,
when it was his personal thoughts
that were disrupting the community.

His crown slid crooked on his head.
He put it straight, but the crown went
awry again. Eight times this happened.

Finally he began to talk to his headpiece.
"Why do you keep tilting over my eyes?"

"I have to. When your power loses compassion,
I have to show what such a condition looks like."

Immediately Solomon recognized the truth.
He knelt and asked forgiveness.
The crown centered itself on his crown.

When something goes wrong, accuse yourself first.
Even the wisdom of Plato or Solomon
can wobble and go blind.

Listen when your crown reminds you
of what makes you cold toward others,
as you pamper the greedy energy inside.

THE FAR MOSQUE

The place that Solomon made to worship in,
called the Far Mosque, is not built of earth
and water and stone, but of intention and wisdom
and mystical conversation and compassionate action.

Every part of it is intelligence and responsive
to every other. The carpet bows to the broom.
The door knocker and the door swing together
like musicians. This heart sanctuary *does*
exist, but it can't be described. Why try!

Solomon goes there every morning and gives guidance
with words, with musical harmonies, and in actions,
which are the deepest teaching. A prince is just
a conceit until he *does* something with generosity.

A bird delegation came to Solomon complaining,
"Why is it you never criticize the nightingale?"

"Because my way," the nightingale explained
for Solomon, "is different. Mid-March
to mid-June I sing. The other

nine months, while you
continue chirping,
I'm silent."

18 ⁀ The Three Fish:
Gamble Everything for Love

ON GAMBLING

*To a frog that's never left his pond the ocean seems like a gamble.
Look what he's giving up: security, mastery of his world, recognition!
The ocean frog just shakes his head. "I can't really explain what it's
like where I live, but someday I'll take you there."*

⁀

If you want what visible reality
can give, you're an employee.

If you want the unseen world,
you're not living your truth.

Both wishes are foolish,
but you'll be forgiven for forgetting
that what you really want is
love's confusing joy.

⁀

Gamble everything for love,
if you're a true human being.

If not, leave
this gathering.

Half-heartedness doesn't reach
into majesty. You set out
to find God, but then you keep

stopping for long periods
at mean-spirited roadhouses.

In a boat down a fast-running creek,
it feels like trees on the bank
are rushing by. What seems

to be changing around us
is rather the speed of our craft
leaving this world.

THE THREE FISH

This is the story of the lake and the three big fish
that were in it, one of them intelligent,
another half-intelligent,

and the third, stupid.

Some fishermen came to the edge of the lake
with their nets. The three fish saw them.

The intelligent fish decided at once to leave,
to make the long, difficult trip to the ocean.

He thought,

"I won't consult with these two on this.
They will only weaken my resolve, because they love
this place so. They call it *home*. Their ignorance
will keep them here."

When you're traveling, ask a traveler for advice,
not someone whose lameness keeps him in one place.

Muhammad says,

"Love of one's country

is part of the faith."
                        But don't take that literally!
Your real "country" is where you're heading,
not where you *are*.
Don't misread that *hadith*.

In the ritual ablutions, according to tradition,
there's a separate prayer for each body part.
When you snuff water up your nose to cleanse it,
beg for the scent of the spirit. The proper prayer is,
"Lord, wash me. My hand has washed this part of me,
but my hand can't wash my spirit.

                        I can wash this skin,
but you must wash *me*."

A certain man used to say the wrong prayer
for the wrong hole. He'd say the nose-prayer
when he splashed his behind. Can the odor of heaven
come from our rumps? Don't be humble with fools.
Don't take pride into the presence of a master.

It's right to love your home place, but first ask,
"Where is that, really?"

The wise fish saw the men and their nets and said,
"I'm leaving."

Ali was told a secret doctrine by Muhammad
and told not to tell it, so he whispered it down
the mouth of a well. Sometimes there's no one to talk to.
You must just set out on your own.

So the intelligent fish made its whole length
a moving footprint and, like a deer the dogs chase,
suffered greatly on its way, but finally made it
to the edgeless safety of the sea.

The half-intelligent fish thought,
                        "My guide
has gone. I ought to have gone with him,
but I didn't, and now I've lost my chance
to escape.

I wish I'd gone with him."
Don't regret what's happened. If it's in the past,
let it go. Don't even *remember* it!

A certain man caught a bird in a trap.
The bird says, "Sir, you have eaten many cows and sheep
in your life, and you're still hungry. The little bit
of meat on my bones won't satisfy you either.
If you let me go, I'll give you three pieces of wisdom.
One I'll say standing on your hand. One on your roof.
And one I'll speak from the limb of that tree."

The man was interested. He freed the bird and let it stand
on his hand.
            "Number One: Do not believe an absurdity,
no matter who says it."

The bird flew and lit on the man's roof. "Number Two:
Do not grieve over what is past. It's over.
Never regret what has happened."

"By the way," the bird continued, "in my body there's a huge
pearl weighing as much as ten copper coins. It was meant
to be the inheritance of you and your children,
but now you've lost it. You could have owned
the largest pearl in existence, but evidently
it was not meant to be."

The man started wailing like a woman in childbirth.
The bird: "Didn't I just say, *Don't grieve
for what's in the past?* And also, *Don't believe
an absurdity?* My entire body doesn't weigh
as much as ten copper coins. How could I have
a pearl that heavy inside me?"

The man came to his senses. "All right.
Tell me Number Three."

"Yes. You've made such good use of the first two!"

Don't give advice to someone who's groggy
and falling asleep. Don't throw seeds on the sand.
Some torn places cannot be patched.

Back to the second fish,
                    the half-intelligent one.
He mourns the absence of his guide for a while,
and then thinks, "What can I do to save myself
from these men and their nets? Perhaps if I pretend
to be already dead!
                    I'll belly up on the surface
and float like weeds float, just giving myself totally
to the water. To die before I die, as Muhammad
said to."
            So he did that.

He bobbed up and down, helpless,
within arm's reach of the fishermen.

"Look at this! The best and biggest fish
is dead."
            One of the men lifted him by the tail,
spat on him, and threw him up on the ground.

He rolled over and over and slid secretly near
the water, and then, back in.

                        Meanwhile,
the third fish, the dumb one, was agitatedly
jumping about, trying to escape with his agility
and cleverness.
                The net, of course, finally closed
around him, and as he lay in the terrible
frying-pan bed, he thought,
                        "If I get out of this,
I'll never live again in the limits of a lake.
Next time, the ocean! I'll make
the infinite my home."

Inside me a hundred beings
are putting their fingers to their lips and saying,
"That's enough for now. Shhhhh." Silence
is an ocean. Speech is a river.

When the ocean is searching for you, don't walk
to the language-river. Listen to the ocean,
and bring your talky business
to an end.

Traditional words are just babbling
in that presence, and babbling is a substitute
for sight. When you sit down beside your beloved,
send the chaperones away, the old women
who brought you together.

When you are mature and with your love,
the love letters and matchmakers
seem irritating.
                    You might read those letters,
but only to teach beginners about love. One who sees
grows silent. When you're with one of those,
be still and quiet, unless he asks you
to talk. Then draw the words out
as I do this poem with Husam,
the radiance of God.
                    I try to stop talking,
but he makes me continue. Husam, if you are in
the vision, why do you want me to say *words?*

Maybe it's like the poet Abu Nuwas,
who said in Arabic,
                    Pour me some wine,
and talk to me about the wine.
                            The cup is at my mouth
  but my ear interrupts,
                    "I want some."

O ear, what you get is the heat.
You turn red with this wine.
                              But the ear says,
"I want more than that!"

                    ✺

When I remember your love,
I weep, and when I hear people
talking of you,
                    something in my chest,
where nothing much happens now,
moves as in sleep.

                    ✺

All our lives we've looked
into each other's faces.
That was the case today too.

How do we keep our love-secret?
We speak from brow to brow
and hear with our eyes.

                    ✺

THE GIFT OF WATER

Someone who doesn't know the Tigris River exists
brings the caliph who lives near the river
a jar of fresh water. The caliph accepts, thanks him,
and gives in return a jar filled with gold coins.

"Since this man has come through the desert,
he should return by water." Taken out by another door,
the man steps into a waiting boat

and sees the wide freshwater of the Tigris.
He bows his head, "What wonderful kindness
that he took my gift."

Every object and being in the universe is
a jar overfilled with wisdom and beauty,
a drop of the Tigris that cannot be contained
by any skin. Every jarful spills and makes the earth
more shining, as though covered in satin.
If the man had seen even a tributary
of the great river, he wouldn't have brought
the innocence of his gift.

Those that stay and live by the Tigris
grow so ecstatic that they throw rocks at the jugs,
and the jugs become perfect!

      They shatter.
The pieces dance, and water . . .

       Do you see?
Neither jar, nor water, nor stone,

        nothing.

You knock at the door of reality,
shake your thought-wings, loosen
your shoulders,

    and open.

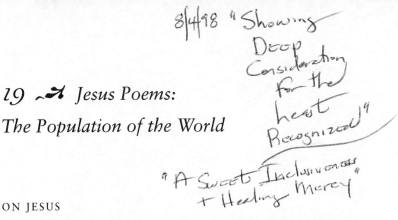

19 ~ Jesus Poems:
The Population of the World

ON JESUS

There's a strong connection between Jesus and Rumi. I'm told a Christian church in Shiraz (Iran) has a quatrain from Rumi carved in stone over its door:

> Where Jesus lives, the great-hearted gather.
> We are a door that's never locked.
>
> If you are suffering any kind of pain,
> stay near this door. Open it.

8/3/98

A sweet inclusiveness and healing mercy are felt around both. The Friendship of Rumi and Shams has no parallel in the great aloneness of Jesus' life, but the relationship with children and with society's outcasts is very similar. Rumi showed deep consideration for the least-recognized members of his thirteenth-century Muslim small town. He would always stop to bow to children and old women, to bless and be blessed by them. One day an Armenian butcher, a Christian, was passing. Rumi stopped in the road and bowed seven times to him. Another day he came upon children playing a game. He acknowledged each as he would have an adult. And there was one little boy far away running across a field. "Wait, I'm coming!" Rumi stayed till the boy had come close, bowed, and been bowed to.

~

I called through your door,
"The mystics are gathering
in the street. Come out!"

"Leave me alone.
I'm sick."

"I don't care if you're dead!"
Jesus is here, and he wants
to resurrect somebody!"

ঌ

JESUS ON THE LEAN DONKEY

Jesus on the lean donkey,
this is an emblem of how the rational intellect
should control the animal-soul.

Let your spirit
be strong like Jesus.

If that part becomes weak,
then the worn-out donkey grows to a dragon.

Be grateful when what seems unkind
comes from a wise person.

Once, a holy man,
riding his donkey, saw a snake crawling into
a sleeping man's mouth! He hurried, but he couldn't
prevent it. He hit the man several blows with his club.

The man woke terrified and ran beneath an apple tree
with many rotten apples on the ground.

"Eat!
You miserable wretch! Eat."

"Why are you doing this to me?"
"Eat more, you fool."

"I've never seen you before!
Who are you? Do you have some inner quarrel with my soul?"

The wise man kept forcing him to eat, and then he ran him.
For hours he whipped the poor man and made him run.
Finally, at nightfall, full of rotten apples,
fatigued, bleeding, he fell

and vomited everything,
the good and the bad, the apples and the snake.

When he saw that ugly snake
come out of himself, he fell on his knees
before his assailant.

"Are you Gabriel? Are you God?

I bless the moment you first noticed me. I was dead
and didn't know it. You've given me a new life.
Everything I've said to you was stupid!
I didn't know."

"If I had explained what I was doing,
you might have panicked and died of fear.
Muhammad said,

'If I described the enemy that lives
inside men, even the most courageous would be paralyzed. No one
would go out, or do any work. No one would pray or fast,
and all power to change would fade
from human beings,'

so I kept quiet
while I was beating you, that like David
I might shape iron, so that, impossibly,
I might put feathers back into a bird's wing.

God's silence is necessary, because of humankind's
faintheartedness. If I had told you about the snake,
you wouldn't have been able to eat, and if
you hadn't eaten, you wouldn't have vomited.

I saw your condition and drove my donkey hard
into the middle of it, saying always under my breath,
'Lord, make it easy on him.' I wasn't permitted
to tell you, and I wasn't permitted to stop
beating you!"

The healed man, still kneeling,
"I have no way to thank you for the quickness
of your wisdom and the strength
of your guidance.

God will thank you."

WHAT JESUS RUNS AWAY FROM

for Todd mercy to Enter if Us the Way to Pop up

The son of Mary, Jesus, hurries up a slope
    as though a wild animal were chasing him.
Someone following him asks, "Where are you going?
    No one is after you." Jesus keeps on,
saying nothing, across two more fields. "Are you
    the one who says words over a dead person,
so that he wakes up?" *I am.* "Did you not make
    the clay birds fly?" *Yes.* "Who then
could possibly cause you to run like this?"
    Jesus slows his pace.

*I say the Great Name over the deaf and the blind,
    they are healed. Over a stony mountainside,
and it tears its mantle down to the navel.
    Over non-existence, it comes into existence.
But when I speak lovingly for hours, for days,
    with those who take human warmth
and mock it, when I say the Name to them, nothing
    happens. They remain rock, or turn to sand,
where no plants can grow. Other diseases are ways
    for mercy to enter, but this non-responding
breeds violence and coldness toward God.
    I am fleeing from that.*

*As little by little air steals water, so praise
    dries up and evaporates with foolish people
who refuse to change. Like cold stone you sit on
    a cynic steals body heat. He doesn't feel
the sun.* Jesus wasn't running from actual people.
    He was teaching in a new way.

꙳

Christ is the population of the world,
and every object as well. There is no room
for hypocrisy. Why use bitter soup for healing
when sweet water is everywhere?

8/4/98

꙳

Lovers think they're looking for each other,
but there's only one search: wandering
this world is wandering that, both inside one
transparent sky. In here
there is no dogma and no heresy.

The miracle of Jesus is himself, not what he said or did
about the future. Forget the future.
I'd worship someone who could do that.

On the way you may want to look back, or not,
but if you can say *There's nothing ahead,*
there will be nothing there.

Stretch your arms and take hold the cloth of your clothes
with both hands. The cure for pain is in the pain.   8/4/98
Good and bad are mixed. If you don't have both,
you don't belong with us.

When one of us gets lost, is not here, he must be inside us.
There's no place like that anywhere in the world.

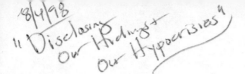
8/4/98
"Disclosing Our Hidings + Our Hypocrisies"

20 ~ In Baghdad, Dreaming of Cairo: More Teaching Stories

ON BAGHDAD

Here are more sections from Rumi's Mathnawi, *the six books of "spiritual couplets" he dictated to his scribe, Husam Chelebi, between 1260 and 1273. Rumi and Husam would walk together around Konya or through the vineyards of Meram nearby, letting the subjects flow into poetry. Passages from the Qur'an, folk tales, jokes, all intrusions were allowed swimming room in this ocean of sublime jazz that perhaps has no parallel in world literature. The Mathnawi is a house of mirrors. Relationship is everywhere, and everywhere we are shown ourselves. The other reveals us. Rumi's stories are full of reflections, comic janitors and stealthy maids, judges and impudent lovers who disclose our hidings and hypocrisies. The whole always throws the parts into relationship, polishing the mirrors. What we see happening in the external drama we can be sure is part of ourselves. It is said that a cow walked across the entire city of Baghdad and saw only some hay that had fallen off a wagon. Likewise, some people travel all around the world and report back that everyone tried to cheat them.*

IN BAGHDAD, DREAMING OF CAIRO: IN CAIRO, DREAMING OF BAGHDAD

No more muffled drums!
Uncover the drumheads!

Plant your flag in an open field!
No more timid peeking around.

Either you see the beloved, 8/4/98
or you lose your head!

If your throat's not ready for that wine, cut it!
If your eyes don't want the fullness of union,
let them turn white with disease.

Either this deep desire of mine
will be found on this journey,
or when I get back home!

It may be that the satisfaction I need
depends on my going away, so that when I've gone
and come back, I'll find it at home.

I will search for the Friend with all my passion
and all my energy, until I learn
that I don't need to search.

The real truth of existence is sealed,
until after many twists and turns of the road.

As in the algebraical method of "the two errors,"
the correct answer comes only after two substitutions,
after two mistakes. Then the seeker says,

"If I had known the real way it was,
I would have stopped all the looking around."

But that knowing depends
on the time spent looking!

Just as the sheikh's debt could not be paid
until the boy's weeping, the story we told in Book II.

You fear losing a certain eminent position.
You hope to gain something from that, but it comes
from elsewhere. Existence does this switching trick,
giving you hope from one source, then
satisfaction from another.
                        It keeps you bewildered
and wondering, and lets your trust in the unseen grow.

You think to make your living from tailoring,
but then somehow money comes in
through goldsmithing,
which had never entered your mind.

I don't know whether the union I want will come
through my effort, or my giving up effort,
or from something completely separate
from anything I do or don't do.

I wait and fidget and flop about
as a decapitated chicken does, knowing that
the vital spirit has to escape this body
eventually, somehow!

This desire will find an opening.

There was once a man
who inherited a lot of money and land.

But he squandered it all too quickly. Those who inherit
wealth don't know what work it took to get it.

In the same way, we don't know the value of our souls,
which were given to us for nothing!

So the man was left alone without provisions,
an owl in the desert.
                    The Prophet has said
that a true seeker must be completely empty like a lute
to make the sweet music of *Lord, Lord.*

When the emptiness starts to get filled with something,
the one who plays the lute puts it down
and picks up another.

There is nothing more subtle and delightful
than to make that music.
                    Stay empty and held
between those fingers, where *where*
gets drunk with nowhere.
                    This man was empty,
and the tears came. His habitual stubbornness
dissolved. This is the way with many seekers.

They moan in prayer, and the perfumed smoke of that
floats into heaven, and the angels say, "Answer
this prayer. This worshiper has only you
and nothing else to depend on. Why do you go first
to the prayers of those less devoted?"

God says,

"By deferring my generosity I am helping him.
His need dragged him by the hair into my presence.
If I satisfy that, he'll go back to being absorbed
in some idle amusement. Listen how passionate he is!
That torn-open cry is the way he should live."

Nightingales are put in cages
because their songs give pleasure.
Whoever heard of keeping a crow?

When two people, one decrepit and the other young
and handsome, come into a bakery where the baker
is an admirer of young men, and both of them
ask for bread, the baker will immediately
give what he has on hand to the old man.

But to the other he will say, "Sit down and wait awhile.
There's fresh bread baking in the house. Almost ready!"

And when the hot bread is brought, the baker will say,
"Don't leave. The halvah is coming!"

So he finds ways of detaining the young man with,
"Ah, there's something important I want to tell you about.
Stay. I'll be back in a moment. Something very important!"

This is how it is when true devotees
suffer disappointment
in the good they want to do,
or the bad they want to avoid.

So this man with nothing, who had inherited everything
and squandered it, kept weeping, *Lord, Lord!*

Finally in a dream he heard a voice, "Your wealth
is in Cairo. Go there to such and such a spot
and dig, and you'll find what you need."

So he left on the long journey,
and when he saw the towers of Cairo,
he felt his back grow warm with new courage.

But Cairo is a large city,
and before he could find the spot,
he had to wander about.

He had no money, of course, so he begged
among the townspeople, but he felt ashamed doing that.
He decided, "I will go out at night
and call like the night-mendicants that people
throw coins into the street for."

                   Shame and dignity and hunger
were pushing him forward and backward and sideways!

Suddenly, he was seized by the night patrol.
It so happened that many had been robbed recently
in Cairo at night, and the caliph had told the police
to assume that anyone out roaming after dark
was a thief.

       It's best not to let offenders go unpunished.
Then they poison the whole body of society. Cut off
the snakebitten finger! Don't be sympathetic
with thieves. Consider instead
the public suffering. In those days
robbers were expert, and numerous!

So the night patrol grabbed the man.
                  "Wait!
I can explain!"
       "Tell me."
                "I am not a criminal.
I am new to Cairo. I live in Baghdad." He told the story
of his dream and the buried treasure,
and he was so believable in the telling that
the night patrolman began to cry. Always,
the fragrance of truth has that effect.

                  Passion
can restore healing power, and prune the weary boughs

to new life. The energy of passion is everything!

There are fake satisfactions that simulate passion.
They taste cold and delicious,
but they just distract you and prevent you
from the search. They say,
                              "I will relieve your passion.
Take me. Take me!"
                              Run from false remedies
that dilute your energy. Keep it rich and musky.

The night patrol said, "I know you're not a thief.
You're a good man, but you're kind of a fool.
I've had that dream before.
                              I was told, in my dream,
that there was a treasure for me in Baghdad,
buried in a certain quarter of the city
on such and such a street."
                              The name of the street
that he said was where this man lived!
                              "And the dream-
voice told me, 'It's in So-and-so's house.
Go there and get it!'"
                              Without knowing,
he had described the exact house,
and mentioned this man's name!
                              "But I didn't do
what the dream said to do, and look at you,
who did, wandering the world, fatigued,
and begging in the streets!"
                              So it came quietly
to the seeker, though he didn't say it out loud,
"What I'm longing for lived in my house in Baghdad!"

He filled with joy. He breathed continuous praise.
Finally he said,
                              "The water of life is here.
I'm drinking it. But I had to come
this long way to know it!"

A lover was telling his beloved
how much he loved her, how faithful
he had been, how self-sacrificing, getting up
at dawn every morning, fasting, giving up
wealth and strength and fame,
all for her.

There was a fire in him.
He didn't know where it came from,
but it made him weep and melt like a candle.

"You've done well," she said, "but listen to me.
All this is the decor of love, the branches
and leaves and blossoms. You must live
at the root to be a true lover."

                              "Where is that!
Tell me!"
                "You've done the outward acts,
but you haven't died. You must die."

When he heard that, he lay back on the ground
laughing, and died. He opened like a rose
that drops to the ground and died laughing.

That laughter was his freedom,
and his gift to the eternal.

As moonlight shines back at the sun,
he heard the call to come home, and went.

When light returns to its source,
it takes nothing
of what it has illuminated.

It may have shone on a garbage dump, or a garden,
or in the center of a human eye. No matter.

It goes, and when it does,
the open plain becomes passionately desolate,
wanting it back.

They were outdoors in some sort of fake
spiritual state, the hypocrite
and his friend, the mayor.

It was midnight, and raining.
A wolf appeared on the edge of the hill.
The mayor let fly an arrow that felled the wolf,
who moaned and farted
and died.

The hypocrite yelled, "You've killed my donkey.
I know my donkey's farts as well as I know
water from wine."
                              "Not so. I shot a wolf.
Go and see. It's too dark to tell anything
from here."
                    "Among twenty farts from twenty animals,
I would know the wind from my young donkey.
Some things I know perfectly."
                                        "You impostor!
In the rain, at midnight, at fifty yards,
you can distinguish one fart from another!
You didn't even recognize me today,
and we've known each other for ten years!

You're just pretending with this God-drunkenness too,
so I guess you'll be excused for other forgetfulnesses,
as a child is, or someone truly dissolved in that joy.
You're not. You're too proud of your 'dervishhood,'
and your cries of 'selfless surrender.'
                                        'O, both worlds
are here! I can't tell which is which!
My donkey's farts prove the sensitivity of my state!'"

This is the way hypocrisy gets exposed.
Anyone who claims, "I am the keeper of the doorway,"
will be tested by the adepts,
                                        as when some fellow claims
to be a tailor, but when the king throws down

a piece of satin and says,
                    "Make me a vest,"
he has no idea what to do.
                        The wine God loves
is human honesty.
                        That hypocrite had been drinking
buttermilk. He was saying, "Leave me alone
in my bewilderment. I don't know a hatchet
from a key. I am Junnaiyd. I am Bestami!"
Spiritual sloth and spiritual greed
will not stay hidden.

If you pretend to be Hallaj
and with that fake burning
set fire to your friends,
don't think that you're a lover.

You're crazy and numb.
You're drinking our blood,
and you have no experience
of the nearness.

DALQAK'S MESSAGE

The King of Tirmid
has urgent business in Samarcand.

He needs a courier to go there and return
in five days. He offers many rewards to anyone
who will make the journey—horses, servants, gold,
and the robes of honor.
                        Dalqak, the court clown,
is out in the country when he hears of this.
He quickly mounts a horse and rides toward town.
He rides furiously. Two horses drop dead
of exhaustion under his whip.
                        He arrives
covered with dust at some ungodly hour,
demanding an audience with the king.

A panic sweeps the city. What calamity
could be imminent that Dalqak, the buffoon,
should be so distraught? Everyone gathers
at the palace.

               "An evil omen is upon us!"
"Something has certainly been spilled on the rug
this time!"

               The king himself is worried.
"What is it, Dalqak?"

                           Whenever anyone asks Dalqak
for particulars about anything, he first puts his finger
to his lips,

            Shhhhh . . .

                    Everyone gets very quiet.
Dalqak makes another gesture as though to say
he needs more time to catch his breath.

Another long wait. No one has ever seen Dalqak
like this. Usually, he's a constant stream
of new jokes. Usually, the king would be
laughing so hard he'd fall on the floor
holding his stomach. This quietness
is very odd and foreboding.

                        Everyone's worst fears
come up.

          "The tyrant from Khwarism
is coming to kill us!"

                "Dalqak, say what it is!"

"I was far from the court when I heard
that you needed a courier, someone who could go
to Samarcand and come back in five days."

                            "Yes!"

"I hurried here to tell you
that I will not be able to do it."

                    "What!"

"I don't have the stamina or the agility.
Don't expect me to be the one."

                  "*This*
is what you made such a commotion about,

that you *won't* do it?"

Dalqak is like those who pretend
to be on a brave spiritual path.

The bridegroom's house
is in an uproar of preparation, always making ready
to receive the bride,
                    but the girl's family
knows nothing. Any message yet?
                              "No."
Any sign of activity?
                    "No."
                              Letters have been written
and sent, but have any of them reached
the Friend? Has your inner
lover read them?

THE CAT AND THE MEAT

There once was a sneering wife
who ate all her husband brought home
and lied about it.

One day it was some lamb for a guest
who was to come. He had worked two hundred days
in order to buy that meat.

When he was away, his wife cooked a kabob
and ate it all, with wine.

The husband returns with the guest.
"The cat has eaten the meat," she says.
"Buy more, if you have any money left!"

He asks a servant to bring the scales,
and the cat. The cat weighs three pounds.
"The meat was three pounds, one ounce.
If this is the cat, where is the meat?
If this is the meat, where is the cat?
Start looking for one or the other!"

If you have a body, where is the spirit?
If you're spirit, what is the body?

This is not our problem to worry about.
Both are both. Corn is corn grain and cornstalk.
The divine butcher cuts us a piece from the thigh,
and a piece from the neck.

Invisible, visible, the world
does not work without both.

If you throw dust at someone's head,
nothing will happen.

If you throw water, nothing.
But combine them into a lump.
                              That marriage
of water and dirt cracks open the head,
and afterward there are other marriages.

SHEIKH KHARRAQANI AND HIS WRETCHED WIFE

Don't look at me.
Fall into the safety of God.
I'm already drowned.
Do I have a beard?
I can't remember.

Rescue this man from his mustache,
curling so proudly, while inside he tears
his hair. Married to God, married
to God, but pretending not!

We see distinctly what this imposture
becomes in a hundred years. A sheikh
looks into a chunk of iron like it's a mirror.
What this bushy-bearded man does not discover in his house
a boy could find so easily.

Dive into the ocean.
You're caught in your own pretentious beard

like something you didn't eat.
You're not garbage! Pearls want to be
like you. You should be with them
where waves and fish and pearls and seaweed and wind
are all one. No linking, no hierarchy,
no distinctions, no perplexed wondering, no speech.
Beyond describing.

Either stay here and talk or go there and be silent.
Or do both, by turns.
With those who see double, talk double-talk.
Make noise, beat a drum, think of metaphors!
With friends, say only mystery.
Near roses, sing.

With deceptive people, cover the jar, and shield it.
But be calm with those in duality.
Speak sweetly and reasonably.
Patience polishes and purifies.

Here's the story of a man looking for Sheikh Kharraqani.

A certain dervish goes out from Talaqan, over the mountains
and through a long valley. The injuries and troubles he suffered
deserve mention, but I'll make it short. The young man
arrives at the sheikh's house and knocks.
The sheikh's wife sticks her head out, "What do you want?"

"I come with the intention of seeing the sheikh."

"Oho," laughs the wife, "look at His Reverence! Was there
nothing to do where you live that you came on such an idle
sight-seeing expedition? Do you hate your hometown? Or maybe
Satan led you here by the nose?" I won't tell you
all she said.

   "Still, I would like to see the sheikh."

"Better you should turn around and go home.
Hundreds of your kind have come like Israelites
to rub their hands on this arrogant gold calf,
parasite, licker-of-platters-on-the-floor,
heavy-slumbering good-for-nothing.

     They say, O,

this is ecstasy, O. They forget any real religious ceremony
and ritual prayers."

              The young man could stand it no more.
"What is this? I've been ambushed by a night patrol
in full daylight! Your blitherings try to keep me
from the presence of a holy man,
but I know what light led me here, the same
that turned the golden calf into words in a sacred story.
A saint is a theater where the qualities of God can be seen.

Don't try to keep me out. Puff on this candle,
and your face will get burned! Rather try blowing out
the sun, or fitting a muzzle on the sea!
Old bats like you dream that their cave-dark
is everywhere, but it's not.

My determination to be in that presence is quick and constant.
You won't stop or slow me.
A revealer of mystery and that which is revealed
are the same. Seed, sowing, growing, harvest, one presence.
The husk, old hag of a nagging world,
should bow to that.

              Hallaj said, *I am God,* and lived it out.
What happens when the I disappears?
What's left after *not?*

Whoever scoffs at these questions and the experiences
they point to, his arrogant spit comes back in his face.
There is no spitting on the way we're on.
Rain itself turns to spit on those who mock
and casually show disrespect to saints."

With that he left the doorway and walked about
asking in the town. Finally someone said, "The *qutb*
is in the forest collecting wood." The young dervish
ran toward the forest but with a doubt,

"Why should such a sheikh have such a woman
for a wife, such an opposite, such a neanderthal!
God forgive my impugning. Who am I
to judge?" But the question remained.

How could a teacher lie with that woman!
Can a guide agree with a thief?

Suddenly Sheikh Kharraqani appears, riding a lion,
firewood stacked behind him. His whip,
a live serpent. Every sheikh rides a fierce lion,
whether you see it or not. Know this
with your other eyes: There are thousands of lions
under your teacher's thighs and all of them
stacked with wood!

Kharraqani knew the problem and immediately began to answer,
"Well, it's not out of desire that I put up with her!
Don't think that. It's not her perfume
or her bright-colored clothes. Enduring her
public disdain has made me strong and patient.
She is my practice. Nothing can be clear
without a polar opposite present. Two banners,
one black, one white, and between them
something gets settled. Between Pharaoh
and Moses, the Red Sea.

You consider issues, but not deeply enough.
Your spring is frozen. Faith is a flowing.
Don't try to forge cold iron.
Study David, the ironsmith, and dancer, and musician.
Move into the sun. You're wrapped in fantasy
and inner mumbling. When spirit enters,
a man begins to wander freely,
escaped and overrunning through the garden plants,
spontaneous and soaking in."

Now a miracle story.

THE SNAKE-CATCHER AND THE FROZEN SNAKE

Listen to this, and hear the mystery inside:
A snake-catcher went into the mountains to find a snake.

He wanted a friendly pet, and one that would amaze
audiences, but he was looking for a reptile, something

that has no knowledge of friendship.

It was winter.
In the deep snow he saw a frighteningly huge dead snake.
He was afraid to touch it, but he did.
In fact, he dragged the thing into Baghdad,
hoping people would pay to see it.

This is how foolish
we've become! A human being is a mountain range!
Snakes are fascinated by us! Yet we sell ourselves
to look at a dead snake.

We are like beautiful satin
used to patch burlap. "Come see the dragon I killed,
and hear the adventures!" That's what he announced,
and a large crowd came,

but the dragon was not dead,
just dormant! He set up his show at a crossroads.
The ring of gawking people got thicker, everybody
on tiptoe, men and women, noble and peasant, all
packed together unconscious of their differences.
It was like the Resurrection!

He began to unwind the thick ropes and remove
the cloth coverings he'd wrapped it so well in.

Some little movement.

The hot Iraqi sun had woken
the terrible life. The people nearest started screaming.
Panic! The dragon tore easily and hungrily
loose, killing many instantly.

The snake-catcher stood there,
frozen. "What have I brought out of the mountains?" The snake
braced against a post and crushed the man and consumed him.

The snake is your animal-soul. When you bring it
into the hot air of your wanting-energy, warmed
by that and by the prospect of power and wealth,
it does massive damage.

Leave it in the snow mountains.
Don't expect to oppose it with quietness
and sweetness and wishing.

The *nafs* don't respond to those,

and they can't be killed. It takes a Moses to deal
with such a beast, to lead it back, and make it lie down
in the snow. But there was no Moses then.
Hundreds of thousands died.

POLISHING THE MIRROR

When Abu Bakr met Muhammad, he said,
"This is not a face that lies."

Abu Bakr was one whose bowl
has fallen from the roof.

There's no hiding the fragrance that comes
from an ecstatic. A polished mirror
cannot help reflecting.

Muhammad once was talking to a crowd
of chieftains, princes with great influence,
when a poor blind man interrupted him.

Muhammad frowned and said to the man,
"Let me attend to these visitors.
This is a rare chance,
whereas you are already my friend.
We'll have ample time."

Then someone nearby said, "That blind man
may be worth a hundred kings. Remember
the proverb, *Human beings are mines.*"

World-power means nothing. Only the unsayable,
jeweled inner life matters.

Muhammad replied, "Do not think that I'm concerned
with being acknowledged by these authorities.

If a beetle moves toward rosewater, it proves
that the solution is diluted. Beetles
love dung, not rose essence.

If a coin is eager to be tested
by the touchstone, that coin
itself may be a touchstone.

A thief loves the night.
I am day. I reveal essences.

A calf thinks God is a cow.
A donkey's theology changes
when someone new pets it
and gives what it wants.

I am not a cow, or thistles for camels
to browse on. People who insult me
are only polishing the mirror."

ALI IN BATTLE

Learn from Ali how to fight
without your ego participating.

God's Lion did nothing
that didn't originate
from his deep center.

Once in battle he got the best of a certain knight
and quickly drew his sword. The man,
helpless on the ground, spat
in Ali's face. Ali dropped his sword,
relaxed, and helped the man to his feet.

"Why have you spared me?
How has lightning contracted back
into its cloud? Speak, my prince,
so that my soul can begin to stir
in me like an embryo."

Ali was quiet and then finally answered,
"I am God's Lion, not the lion of passion.
The sun is my lord. I have no longing
except for the One.

When a wind of personal reaction comes,
I do not go along with it.

There are many winds full of anger,
and lust and greed. They move the rubbish
around, but the solid mountain of our true nature
stays where it's always been.

There's nothing now
except the divine qualities.
Come through the opening into me.

Your impudence was better than any reverence,
because in this moment I am you and you are me.

I give you this opened heart as God gives gifts:
the poison of your spit has become
the honey of friendship."

21 ✌ Beginning and End:
The Stories That Frame the Mathnawi

ON THE FRAME

Like other artworks born of a spiritual impulse, Rumi's Mathnawi
*demolishes its form and overreaches its boundaries. Yet two extended
stories, near the beginning of Book I and near the end of Book VI,
give a kind of rounded effect to the whole. They are love stories.
In both, the narrow romantic love changes to ecstatic love of the
beloved, and in both there is a disturbing act of violence (the poison-
ing of the goldsmith and the killing of the second brother) that is cru-
cial to the Khidresque mystery. The* Mathnawi *itself is a love story
that obliterates lovers. "Don't look for me in a human shape." These
are two stories of that difficult truth: How wanting the Chinese
princess leads into the mystery of* Die before you die. *How a picture,
an appearance, starts us, the king's three sons, out on a path to the
formless marriage. It's overstating the point to say that the stories
"frame" the* Mathnawi. *Where the refrain "This never ends" keeps
revolving by, no model of linear structure is appropriate.*

THE KING AND THE HANDMAIDEN AND THE DOCTOR

Do you know why your soul-mirror
does not reflect as clearly as it might?

Because rust has begun to cover it.
It needs to be cleaned.
                    Here's a story
about the inner state that's meant by *soul-mirror.*

In the old days there was a king
who was powerful in both his kingdoms,
the visible as well as the spiritual.

One day as he was riding on the hunt, he saw a girl
and was greatly taken with her beauty.

As was the custom,
he paid her family handsomely and asked that she come
to be a servant at the palace. He was in love with her.

The feelings trembled and flapped in his chest
like a bird newly put in a cage.

But as soon as she arrived, she fell ill.
The king was like the man who had a donkey,
but no saddle for the pack. Then he bought a saddle,
and wolves killed the donkey.

He had a waterjar,
but no water. Then he found water, but the pitcher
fell and broke.

He brought his doctors together.
"You have both our lives in your hands. Her life
is my life. Whoever heals her will receive
the finest treasure I have, the coral inlaid
with pearls, anything!"

"We'll do what we can. Each of us
is the healing-savior of our regions. Surely
we can find a cure."

They neglected, in the pride
of their accomplishments, to say *If God wills.*
I don't mean that just the *saying* of the phrase
would have helped.

There was a coldness and a closed
quality beneath the omission. There are many
who don't say *Inshallah,* and yet their whole soul
resonates with it all the time!

So the doctors began,
and no matter what they tried, the girl got more pale
and thin. The effects of their medicines were
the opposite of what they expected.

Oxymel
produced bile. Almond oil caused dryness. Myrobalen,
instead of loosening the bowels, constricted them.

Water seemed to feed the fever.

                              The king saw
that his doctors were helpless. He ran barefooted
to the mosque. He knelt on the prayer rug
and soaked the point of it with his tears.

He dissolved into an annihilated state,
and as he came out of that, he spoke this prayer:

"You know what's hidden here. I don't know what to do.
You have said, 'Even though I know all secrets,
still declare it outwardly with an action.'"

He cried out loud for help, and the ocean of grace
surged over him. He slept in the midst
of his weeping on the prayer rug.

In his dream an old man appeared.

                              "Good king,
I have news. Tomorrow a stranger will come.
I have sent him. He is a physician you can trust.
Listen to him."

                     As dawn came, the king was sitting up
in the belvedere on his roof. He saw someone coming,
a person like the dawn. He ran to meet this guest.

Like two swimmers who love the water, their souls knit
together without being sewn, no seam.

                              The king said,
"You are my beloved, not the girl! But actions
spring from actions in this reality.
What should I do?"

                     We should always ask for discipline.
One who has no self-control cannot receive grace.

And it's not just himself he hurts. Undisciplined
people set fire to the landscape!

                              A table of food
was once coming down from the sky to feed Moses
and his people, when suddenly voices from the crowd
called out, "Where's the garlic?"

and "We want lentils!"

                    At once the bread and the dishes
of grace-food disappeared. Everyone had to keep digging
with mattocks and cutting with long scythes.

Then Jesus interceded and sent more trays of food.
But again some insolent people showed no respect.
They grabbed like it wouldn't be enough,

                              even though Jesus
kept telling them, "This food will last.
It will always be here."

                    To be suspicious and greedy
when majesty arrives is the worst arrogance.
The gates closed.

              Withhold your giving, and no
rainclouds will form. When sex goes on between
everybody all the time, epidemics spread
in every direction.

                    When you feel gloomed over,
it's your failure to praise. Irreverence
and no discipline rob your soul of light.

                              The king opened
his arms and held the saintly doctor to him. He kissed
his hand and his forehead and asked how his journey
had been. Many dear concerns for this one
who had been announced in his dream.
He led him to the head table.

"At last, I have found what patience can bring.
This one whose face answers any question, who simply
by looking can loosen the knot of intellectual discussion.

You translate what is inside us.
If you were to vanish, this vast meeting room
would shrink to a closet. Protect us."

They talked and ate a spirit meal. Then the king
took the doctor's hand and led him to where
the girl lay, telling him the story
of her illness.

              The doctor felt her pulse

and observed her coloring and her urine. "Your healers
have not helped. They've made her worse.
They don't know the inner states."

The secret
of her pain opened to him, but he didn't tell the king
what it was. It was love, of course.

The ailments of love are different from any other.
Love is the astrolabe that sights into the mysteries
of God.

Earth-love, spirit-love, any love
looks into that yonder, and whatever I try to say
explaining love is embarrassing!

Some commentary
clarifies, but with love silence is clearer.
A pen went scribbling along, but when it tried
to write *love*, it broke.

If you want to expound on love,
take your intellect out and let it lie down
in the mud. It's no help.

You want proof that the sun exists, so you stay up
all night talking about it. Finally you sleep
as the sun comes up.

Look at it! Nothing
is so strange in this entire world as the sun.
The sun of the soul is even more so. It has no yesterday!
The physical sun is unique, but it's possible
to imagine something like it.

The spiritual sun
has nothing comparable, inner or outer.
Imagination cannot contain it. Word of that
sun, Shams, came,

and everything hid. Now Husam
touches my arm. He wants me to say more about Shams.

Not now, Husam. I don't know how to make words make
sense, or praise. In the Friend-place nothing true
can be *said*. Let me just be here.

But Husam begs,
"Feed me! Hurry! Time is a sharp downstroke. A sufi

is supposed to be a child of the moment. Aren't you
a sufi? Don't say *tomorrow* or *later!*"

                                    And I reply,
"It's better that the way of the Friend be concealed
in a story. Let the mystery come through what
people say around the lovers, not from
what lovers say to each other."

                                    "No! I want this
as naked and true as it can be. I don't wear a shirt
when I lie down with my beloved!"

                                    "O Husam. If the Friend
came to you completely naked, your chest could not stand it.
You wouldn't be here in your body any longer. Ask
for what you want, but within some limits.

A little stick can't hold up a mountain.
If that inner sun by which existence exists
came even a little closer, everything
would be scorched. Don't ask for that.
Say no more for now about Shamsi Tabriz."

                                    This has no end.
Go back to the beginning,

                        the end of the story
of the king and the lovesick maiden
and the holy doctor, who said,

                                    "Leave me alone with the girl."
It was done, and quietly he began.

                                    "Where are you from?
Who are your relatives there? Who else are you close
to in that region?"

                        On and on he gently asked
about her life. When someone steps barefooted on a thorn,
he immediately puts his foot on his knee and searches
with a needle, and when he can't locate the tip,
he moistens around the place with moisture
from his lips. A splinter is often
difficult to get out.

                        How much more difficult a thorn
in the heart! If everyone could find that thorn
in themselves, things would be

much more peaceful here!
                              Someone puts a clump of burrs
under a donkey's tail. The donkey doesn't know
what's wrong. He just starts jumping
and bucking around.
                          An intelligent, thorn-removing
doctor must come and investigate.
                              So the divine physician
asked about her friends and held her hand
to feel the pulse.
                      She told many stories of her home,
mentioning many names, and he would say the names again
after her to test the pulse reaction.
                              Finally he asked,
"When you visit other towns, where are you most likely to go?"
She said one town, then another, where she bought bread
and where salt, describing the houses,
                              until he happened
to say the word *Samarcand!*
                          The dear city sweet as candy.
She blushed. Her breath caught. O she loves
a goldsmith in Samarcand! She misses him so.
                                  "Where *exactly*
does he live?"
                  "At the head of the bridge on Ghatafar Street."
"Now I can heal you. Don't be afraid. I will do to you
what rain does to a meadow. But don't tell this
to anyone, certainly not the king.
                              When the love center
in your chest becomes the grave for such a secret,
then what you want will be quickly yours."
                                  Seeds must hide
in the ground to become whatever is in them.
The girl felt better. She trusted him.
                              The doctor
went to the king and told him part of the story.
                                  "On some pretext
we must bring here from Samarcand a certain goldsmith.
Lure him with the prospect of wealth and honors."

The king's messengers went with robes and coins
and easily persuaded the man to leave
his family and his town.

                            He rode an Arabian horse
into the presence of the king and the doctor,
who said,

                "Marry the girl to this man,
and she will be completely cured."

                                It was done,
and for six months those two loved and made love
and totally satisfied themselves with each other.
The girl was restored to perfect health.

Then the physician gave the goldsmith a potion,
so that he began to sicken.

                            His handsomeness faded,
and his strength dwindled. Little by little he became
sunken-cheeked and jaundiced and ugly,

                                        and the girl stopped
loving him. Any love based on physical beauty
is not love.

                "This world is a mountain. What we do
is a shout. The echo comes back to us."

                                        The goldsmith said
that and died. Choose to love the one
who does not die.

                        Don't say, "But how can we *do* that?"
The generous one is not hard to find.

                                    But what about
the doctor's poisoning the poor goldsmith! It was not done
for the king's sake. The reason is a mystery
like Khidr's cutting the boy's throat.

                            Everything
the doctor did was out of God's will. Khidr
sunk the boat, yet it was right to do.

                                When someone
is killed by a doctor like this one, it's a blessing,
even though it might not seem so.

                            A child cries
at its first haircut, but not the mother. Such a doctor

is part of a larger generosity. He takes away one
and gives back a hundred.

> Don't judge his actions
by what you would do. You are not living
completely within truth as he is.

THE THREE BROTHERS AND THE CHINESE PRINCESS

There was a king who had three
equally accomplished sons.

Each was generous and wise, and fiercely
decisive when the need arose.

They stood like three strongly burning candles
before their father, ready to set out on a journey
to distant parts of his kingdom to see
if they were being administered fairly and well.

Each kissed the king's hand as a sign
of farewell and obedience.

"Go wherever you are drawn to go," said the king,
"and dance on your way.

> You are protected.
I only warn you not to enter one particular
castle, the one called *The Fortress
That Takes Away Clarity.*

That castle has a gallery of beautiful pictures
which causes great difficulty for the royal family.
It's like the chamber Zuleikha decorated to trap Joseph,
where her picture was everywhere.

> He could not avoid
looking at her. Stay away from that one place."

Of course, as it happens, the three princes
were obsessed with seeing *that* castle, and in spite
of their father's admonition they went
into it.

> It had five gates facing the land and five

facing the ocean, as the five external senses
take in the color and perfume of phenomena
and the five inner senses open onto the mystery.

The thousands of pictures there made the princes
restless. They wandered the hallways drunkenly,
until they came,

          all three at the same time,
to stand before a particular portrait,

                    a woman's face.
They fell hopelessly in love. "This is what our father
warned us of. We thought we were strong enough
to resist anything, as one who has phthisis
thinks he's well enough to go on,

                but we're not!
Who is this?"

          A wise sheikh revealed to them, "She
is the Chinese princess, the hidden one.
The Chinese king has concealed her as the spirit
is wrapped in an embryo. No one may come
into her presence.

          Birds are not even allowed
to fly over her roof. No one can figure a way in.
She can't be won by contriving. Give up on that!"

The princes put their heads together anyway,
comrades in one sighing passion.

The oldest said, "We've always been bold
when we gave counsel to others, but look at us!
We used to say, *Patience is the key,* but the rules
we made for others are no help now. We advised, *Laugh!*
Why are we so quiet? Where is our strength?"

                    In despair
they set out for China, not with any hope for a union
with the princess, but just to be closer to her.

They left everything and went toward the hidden beloved.
They lived disguised in the capital, trying
to devise some way into the palace.

Finally the eldest, "I can't wait like this.
I don't want to live if I have to live separated
from the beloved. This is the one
I've been beating the drum for my entire life.

What does a duck care about a shipwreck?
Just the duck's feet in ocean water is ship enough.
My soul and my body are married to this boasting.
I am dreaming but I'm not asleep.
I brag but I do not lie.
                        I'm a candle.
Pass the knife through my neck a hundred times,
I'll burn just as brightly.
                        The haystack of my existence
has caught on both sides. Let it burn all night
down to nothing.
                        On the road the moon gives
all the light I need. I'm going to confront the king
with my desire."
                        His brothers tried to persuade him
not to, but they couldn't. He sprang up
and came staggering into the presence of the Chinese
king, who knew what was happening, though
he kept silent.
                        That king was *inside* the three
brothers, but he pretended to be unfamiliar
with them.
                        The fire under the kettle is the appearance.
The boiling water is the reality.
                        The beloved
is in your veins though he or she may *seem*
to have a form outside you.
                        The prince knelt
and kissed the king's feet, and stayed there,
bowed down.
                        "This young man will have everything
he seeks, and twenty times that which he left
behind. He gambled and flung off his robe
in ecstasy. Such love is worth a thousand robes.

This one is an ambassador from that love,
and he is doing his work well."

The prince heard this
and could not speak, but his soul spoke constantly
with that soul. The prince thought, "*This* is
reality, this waking, this melting away."

He stayed bowed down with the king a long time,
cooking. "Execution is one thing,

but I am being executed
again and again every moment! Poor in wealth,
but rich in lives to sacrifice.

No one can play
the game of love with just one head!"

This joyful waiting
consumed the prince. The *form* of the beloved
left his mind and he found union.

"The clothes of the body were sweet silk,
but this nakedness is sweeter."

This subject can go
no further. What comes next must stay hidden.

One rides
to the ocean on horseback, but after that
the wooden horse of mystical silence
must carry you.

When that boat sinks,
you are the fish, neither silent nor speaking,
a marvel with no name.

So the oldest brother died,
and the middle brother came to the funeral.

"What's this?
A fish from the same sea!" mused the king. The chamberlain
called out, "A son of the same father, the brother
next in age to the deceased."

The king, "Yes, a keepsake
from that one to me."

So the sublime kindnesses
descended again, and the courtyard seemed split apart
like a pomegranate laughing, with all the forms

of the universe opening their tent flaps,
new creations every second.

                      He had read about such
revelations in books. Now it was his. He kept saying,
"Is there more? Is there more?" Fed from the king's nature,
he felt a satisfaction he'd never felt before,
and then there came a pride.

                       "Am I not also a king,
the son of a king? Why is this one controlling *me?*
I should open my own shop, independent of him."

The king thought, "I give you pure light,
and you throw dirt in my face!"
                       The middle brother
suddenly realized what he had inwardly done,
but it was too late.
               His magnificence
was stripped away. No longer a garden peacock,
he flew like a lonely owl in the wilderness,
like Adam plowing an ox far from Eden.

                       He came to himself
and asked forgiveness, and with his repentance
he combined something else, the deep pain
that comes from losing the union.
                This story must be
shortened. After a year when the king came out
of his own self-effacement, he found one arrow missing
from his quiver and the middle brother dead,
shot through the throat.
                The king wept, both slayer
and chief mourner. Yet all was well. The middle brother too
had gone to the beloved through the killing eye
that blasted his conceit.

It was the third brother,
who had been ill up until now,
who received the hand of the princess.

He lived the marriage of form and spirit,
and did absolutely nothing
to deserve it.

22 ᝰ *Green Ears Everywhere:*
Children Running Through

*In China they tell of three laughing Taoist masters, who taught by
going into town and standing in the marketplace and laughing. One
of them died. People curious as to how the remaining two would act
gathered at the funeral pyre. The other two masters had been given
instructions not to prepare the body in any way, not even to change
the clothes the dead man was wearing. He had crammed his pockets
full of firecrackers. The teaching began again. Rumi's poems are like
firecrackers on a funeral pyre. They won't allow much public postur-
ing, and they point us away from misery.*

ᝰ

I used to be shy.
You made me sing.

I used to refuse things at table.
Now I shout for more wine.

In somber dignity, I used to sit
on my mat and pray.

Now children run through
and make faces at me.

ᝰ

There was a long drought. Crops dried up.
The vineyard leaves turned black.

People were gasping and dying like fish
thrown up on shore and left there.
But one man was always laughing and smiling.

A group came and asked,
"Have you no compassion for this suffering?"

He answered, "To your eyes this is a drought.
To me, it is a form of God's joy.

Everywhere in this desert I see green corn
growing waist high, a sea-wilderness
of young ears greener than leeks.

I reach to touch them.
How could I not?

You and your friends are like Pharaoh
drowning in the Red Sea of your body's blood.
Become friends with Moses, and see this other riverwater."

When you think your father is guilty of an injustice,
his face looks cruel. Joseph, to his envious brothers,
seemed dangerous. When you make peace with your father,
he will look peaceful and friendly. The whole world
is a form for truth.
                    When someone does not feel grateful
to that, the forms appear to be *as he feels*.
They mirror his anger, his greed, and his fear.
Make peace with the universe. Take joy in it.

It will turn to gold. Resurrection
will be now. Every moment,
a new beauty.

And never any boredom!
Instead this abundant, pouring
noise of many springs in your ears.

The tree limbs will move like people dancing,
who suddenly know what the mystical life is.

The leaves snap their fingers like they're hearing music.
They are! A sliver of a mirror shines out
from under a felt covering. Think how it will be
when the whole thing is open to the air and the sunlight!

There are some mysteries that I'm not telling you.
There's so much doubt everywhere, so many opinions
that say, "What you announce may be true
in the future, but not now."
But this form of universal truth that I see
says,

> *This is not a prediction. This is here
> in this instant, cash in the hand!*

This reminds me of the sons of Uzayr,
who were out on the road looking for their father.
They had grown old, and their father had miraculously
grown young! They met him and asked, "Pardon us, sir,
but have you seen Uzayr? We heard that he's supposed
to be coming along this road today."

"Yes," said Uzayr, "he's right behind me."
One of the sons replied, "That's good news!"

The other fell on the ground.
He had recognized his father.

"What do you mean *news!* We're already inside
the sweetness of his presence."

To your minds there is such a thing as *news,*
whereas to the inner knowing, it's all
in the middle of its happening.

To doubters, this is a pain.
To believers, it's gospel.
To the lover and the visionary,
it's life as it's being lived!

The rules of faithfulness
are just the door and the doorkeeper.

They keep the presence from being interrupted.

Being unfaithful is like the outside of a fruit peeling.
It's dry and bitter because it's facing away from the center.
Being faithful is like the inside of the peeling,
wet and sweet. But the place for peelings
is the fire. The real inside is beyond "sweet"
and "bitter." It's the source of deliciousness.

This can't be said. I'm drowning in it!

Turn back! And let me cleave a road through water
like Moses. This much I will say,
and leave the rest hidden:

Your intellect is in fragments, like bits of gold
scattered over many matters. You must scrape them
together, so the royal stamp can be pressed into you.

Cohere, and you'll be as lovely as Samarcand
with its central market, or Damascus. Grain by grain,
collect the parts. You'll be more magnificent
than a flat coin. You'll be a cup
with carvings of the king
around the outside.

The Friend will become bread and springwater for you,
a lamp and a helper, your favorite dessert
and a glass of wine.
                 Union with that one
is grace. Gather the pieces,
so I can show you what is.

That's what talking is for,
to help us to be One. Manyness
is having sixty different emotions.
Unity is peace, and silence.

I know I ought to be silent,
but the excitement of this keeps opening
my mouth as a sneeze or a yawn does.

Muhammad says, *I ask forgiveness seventy times a day,*
and I do the same. Forgive me. Forgive my talking
so much. But the way God makes mysteries *manifest*
quickens and keeps the flow of words in me continual.

A sleeper sleeps while his bedclothes drink in
the riverwater. The sleeper dreams of running around
looking for water and pointing in the dream to mirages,
"Water! There! There!" It's that *There!*
that keeps him asleep. *In the future, in the distance,*
those are illusions. Taste the *here* and the *now* of God.

This present thirst is your real intelligence,
not the back-and-forth, mercurial brightness.
Discursiveness dies and gets put in the grave.

This contemplative joy does not.
Scholarly knowledge is a vertigo,
an exhausted famousness.
Listening is better.

Being a teacher is a form of desire,
a lightning flash. Can you ride to Wahksh,
far up the Oxus River, on a streak of lightning?

Lightning is not guidance.
Lightning simply tells the clouds to weep.
Cry a little. The streak-lightning of our minds
comes so that we'll weep and long for our real lives.

A child's intellect says, "I should go to school."
But that intellect cannot teach itself.

A sick person's mind says, "Go to the doctor,"
but that doesn't cure the patient.

Some devils were sneaking up close to heaven
trying to hear the secrets, when a voice came,
"Get out of here. Go to the world. Listen
to the prophets!" Enter the house through the door.
It's not a long way. You are empty reeds,
but you can become sugarcane again,
if you'll listen to the guide.

When a handful of dirt was taken from the hoofprint
of Gabriel's horse and thrown inside the golden calf,
the calf lowed! That's what the guide can do
for you. The guide can make you *live*.

The guide will take your falcon's hood off.
Love is the falconer, your king.

Be trained by that. Never say, or think,
"I am better than . . . whoever."

That's what Satan thought.
Sleep in the spirit tree's peaceful shade,
and never stick your head out from that green.

❧

Birdsong brings relief
to my longing.

I am just as ecstatic as they are,
but with nothing to say!

Please, universal soul, practice
some song, or something, through me!

❧

The way of love is not
a subtle argument.

The door there
is devastation.

Birds make great sky-circles
of their freedom.
How do they learn it?

They fall, and falling,
they're given wings.

❧

Let your throat-song
be clear and strong enough

to make an emperor fall full-length,
suppliant, at the door.

✒

I have phrases and whole pages memorized,
but nothing can be told of love.

You must wait until you and I
are living together.

In the conversation we'll have
then . . . be patient . . . then.

✒

You've so distracted me,
your absence fans my love.
Don't ask how.

Then you come near.
"Do not . . . ," I say, and
"Do not . . . ," you answer.

Don't ask why
this delights me.

✒

I'M NOT SAYING THIS RIGHT

You bind me, and I tear away in a rage to open out
into air, a round brightness, a candlepoint,
all reason, all love.

This confusing joy, your doing,
this hangover, your tender thorn.

You turn to look, I turn.
I'm not saying this right.

I am a jailed crazy who ties up spirit-women.
I am Solomon.

What goes comes back. Come back.
We never left each other.

A disbeliever hides disbelief,
but I will say his secret.

More and more awake, getting up at night,
spinning and falling with love for Shams.

THE LEAST FIGURE

I tried to think of some way
to let my face become yours.

"Could I whisper in your ear
a dream I've had? You're the only one
I've told this to."

You tilt your head, laughing,
as if, "I know the trick you're hatching,
but go ahead."

I am an image you stitch with gold thread
on a tapestry, the least figure,
a playful addition.

But nothing you work on is dull.
I am part of the beauty.

I reach for a piece of wood. It turns into a lute.
I do some meanness. It turns out helpful.
I say one must not travel during the holy month.
Then I start out and wonderful things happen.

"Convictions Hold ? With Deep Gentleness"

23 ~ Being Woven:
Communal Practice

ON BEING WOVEN

There's a game that's remembered in Iran called moshaereh, *which means "being in company with poetry." One person says a line from Rumi, then the next person must* begin *a Rumi line with the word the first person's ended with. And so on for hours, I'm told, before television deadened the psyche, a family or a group of friends might continue. Rumi was not the only poet used. It might be Hafiz, or Attar, or others. Poetry wove together the fabric of community and kept it lively. We have nothing comparable, except perhaps the nights of trading poems back and forth that sometimes happen in gatherings.*

In December of 1273 when Rumi died, representatives of every major religion came to his funeral. In the midst of the crusades and violent sectarian conflict he said, "I go into the Muslim mosque and the Jewish synagogue and the Christian church and I see one altar." And he made it clear in other places that someone who considers religion or nation an important human category is in danger of severing the heart from its ability to act compassionately. This is a radical idea now, but Rumi held the conviction in the thirteenth century with such deep gentleness that its truth was recognized.

OF BEING WOVEN

"The way is full of genuine sacrifice.

The thickets blocking the path are anything
that keeps you from that, any fear
that you may be broken to bits like a glass bottle.
This road demands courage and stamina,

yet it's full of footprints! Who *are*
these companions? They are rungs
in your ladder. Use them!
With company you quicken your ascent.

You may be happy enough going along,
but with others you'll get farther, and faster.

Someone who goes cheerfully by himself
to the customs house to pay his traveler's tax
will go even more lightheartedly
when friends are with him.

Every prophet sought out companions.
A wall standing alone is useless,
but put three or four walls together,
and they'll support a roof and keep
the grain dry and safe.

When ink joins with a pen, then the blank paper
can say something. Rushes and reeds must be *woven*
to be useful as a mat. If they weren't interlaced,
the wind would blow them away.
                    Like that, God paired up   8/5/98
creatures, and gave them friendship."

This is how the fowler and the bird were arguing
about hermitic living and Islam.

It's a prolonged debate.
Husam, shorten their controversy.
Make the *Mathnawi* more nimble and less lumbering.
Agile sounds are more appealing to the heart's ear.

THE WATERWHEEL

Stay together, friends.
Don't scatter and sleep.

Our friendship is made
of being awake.

The waterwheel accepts water
and turns and gives it away,
weeping.

That way it stays in the garden,
whereas another roundness rolls
through a dry riverbed looking
for what it thinks it wants.

Stay here, quivering with each moment
like a drop of mercury.

THE GRANARY FLOOR

A sufi was wandering the world.
One night he came as a guest to a community of sufis.
He tied up his donkey in the stable
and then was welcomed to the head of the dais.
They went into deep meditation and mystical communion,
he and these friends. For such people
a person's presence is more to learn from
than a book. A sufi's book is not composed
with ink and alphabet. A scholar loves, and lives on,
the marks of a pen. A sufi loves footprints!
He sees those and stalks his game. At first, he *sees*
the clues. After a time he can follow the scent.
To go guided by fragrance is a hundred times better
than following tracks. A person who is opening
to the divine is like a door to a sufi.
What might appear a worthless stone
to others, to him's a pearl. You see your image
clearly in a mirror. A sheikh sees more than that
in a discarded brick. Sufi masters are those
whose spirits existed before the world.
Before the body, they lived many lifetimes.

Before seeds went into the ground, they harvested wheat.
Before there was an ocean, they strung pearls.
While the great meeting was going on about bringing

human beings into existence, they stood up to their chins
in wisdom water. When some of the angels opposed
creation, the sufi sheikhs laughed and clapped
among themselves. Before materiality, they knew
what it was like to be trapped inside matter.
Before there was a nightsky, they saw Saturn.
Before wheat grains, they tasted bread.
With no mind, they thought.

Immediate intuition to them is the simplest act
of consciousness, what to others would be epiphany.
Much of our thought is of the past, or the future.
They're free of those. Before a mine is dug,
they judge coins. Before vineyards,
they know the excitements to come.
In July, they feel December.
In unbroken sunlight, they find shade. In *fana,*
the state where all objects dissolve,
they recognize objects. The open sky drinks
from their circling cup. The sun wears
the gold of their generosity.

When two of them meet, they are no longer two.
They are one and six hundred thousand.
The ocean waves are their closest likeness,
when wind makes, from unity, the numerous.
This happened to the sun, and it broke into rays
through the window, into bodies.
The disc of the sun does exist, but if you see
only the ray-bodies, you may have doubts.
The human-divine combination is a oneness.
Plurality, the apparent separation into rays.

Friend, we're traveling together.
Throw off your tiredness. Let me show you
one tiny spot of the beauty that cannot be spoken.
I'm like an ant that's gotten into the granary,
ludicrously happy, and trying to lug out
a grain that's way too big.

A SONG ABOUT A DONKEY

The following is about the dangers
of imitating others in your spiritual life.

Meet the Friend on your own.
Try to dissolve out of selfishness
into a voice beyond those limits.

A wandering sufi came with his donkey
to a community of sufis who were very poor.
He fed the donkey and gave it water,
left it with his servant, and went inside.

Immediately, a group of the resident sufis
sold the donkey and bought food and candles
for a feast.
                        There was jubilation in the monastery!
No more patience and three-day fasting!

If you are rich and full-fed, don't laugh
at the impulsiveness of the poor.
They were not acting from their souls,
but they were acting out of some necessity.

The traveler joined in the festivities.
They paid constant attention to him,
caressing him, honoring him.
                                    The *sema* began.
There was smoke from the kitchen,
dust from the feet hitting the floor,
and ecstasy from the longing of the dancers.

Their hands were waving.
Their foreheads swept low across the dais.
It had been a long wait for such an occasion.

Sufis always have to wait a long time
for their desire. That's why they're such
great eaters!
                        The sufi who feeds on light, though,
is different, but there's only one of those

in a thousand. The rest live under
that one's protection.

The *sema* ran its course
and ended. The poet began to sing a deep grief song,
"The donkey is gone, my son. Your donkey is gone."

Everyone joined in, clapping their hands and singing
over and over, "The donkey is gone, my son.
Your donkey is gone."

And the visiting sufi
sang more passionately than all the rest. Finally,
it was dawn, and they parted with many good-byes.
The banquet room was empty. The man brought out
his baggage and called to his servant,
"Where's my donkey?"

"Look at you!"

"What do you mean?"

"They sold your donkey! That's how we had
such a celebration!"

"Why didn't you come and tell me?"

"Several times I came near, but you were always
singing so loudly, 'The donkey's gone,
the donkey's gone,' that I thought you knew.
I thought you had a secret insight."

"Yes.
It was my imitation of their joy that caused this."

Even the good delight of friends is at first
a reflection in you. Stay with them
until it becomes a realization.

The imitation here
came from the man's desire to be honored.
It deafened him to what was being
so constantly said.

Remember there's only one reason
to do anything: a meeting with the Friend
is the only real payment.

Some Hindus have an elephant to show.
No one here has ever seen an elephant.
They bring it at night to a dark room.

One by one, we go in the dark and come out
saying how we experience the animal.

One of us happens to touch the trunk.
"A water-pipe kind of creature."

Another, the ear. "A very strong, always moving
back and forth, fan-animal."

Another, the leg. "I find it still,
like a column on a temple."

Another touches the curved back.
"A leathery throne."

Another, the cleverest, feels the tusk.
"A rounded sword made of porcelain."
He's proud of his description.

Each of us touches one place
and understands the whole in that way.

The palm and the fingers feeling in the dark are
how the senses explore the reality of the elephant.

If each of us held a candle there,
and if we went in together,
we could see it.

24 ⁊ Wished-For Song:
Secret Practices

8/4/98

ON SECRECY

The egg is Rumi's image for the private place where each individual globe of soul fruit becomes elaborately unique. Incubation in secret practices produces the lovely differences. Out of one leathery egg, a sparrow, out of a similar one, a snake. Transformations that happen on retreat, the forty-day chilla, *are comparable to the changes that come during nine months in a human womb. Meditation, or any solitary practice (a walk before dawn, a poem every morning, sitting on the roof at sunset), gives depth and expands the soul's action.*

A man in prison is sent a prayer rug by his friend. What he had wanted, of course, was a file or a crowbar or a key! But he began using the rug, doing five-times prayer before dawn, at noon, mid-afternoon, after sunset, and before sleep. Bowing, sitting up, bowing again, he notices an odd pattern in the weave of the rug, just at the qibla, *the point, where his head touches. He studies and meditates on that pattern, gradually discovering that it is a diagram of the lock that confines him in his cell and how it works. He's able to escape. Anything you do every day can open into the deepest spiritual place, which is freedom.*

A WISHED-FOR SONG

You're song,
a wished-for song.

Go through the ear to the center
where sky is, where wind,
where silent knowing.

Put seeds and cover them.
Blades will sprout
where you do your work.

A BASKET OF FRESH BREAD

The Prophet Muhammad said,

"There is no better companion
on this way than what you do. Your actions will be
your best friend, or if you're cruel and selfish,
your actions will be a poisonous snake
that lives in your grave."

But tell me,
can you do the good work without a teacher?
Can you even know what it is without the presence
of a Master? Notice how the lowest livelihood
requires some instruction.

First comes knowledge,
then the doing of the job. And much later,
perhaps after you're dead, something grows
from what you've done.

Look for help and guidance
in whatever craft you're learning. Look for a generous
teacher, one who has absorbed the tradition he's in.

Look for pearls in oyster shells.
Learn technical skill from a craftsman.

Whenever you meet genuine spiritual teachers,
be gentle and polite and fair with them.
Ask them questions, and be eager
for answers. Never condescend.

If a master tanner wears an old, threadbare smock,
that doesn't diminish his mastery.

If a fine blacksmith works at the bellows
in a patched apron, it doesn't affect
how he bends the iron.

Strip away your pride,

and put on humble clothes.

If you want to learn theory,
talk with theoreticians. That way is oral.

When you learn a craft, practice it.
That learning comes through the *hands*.

If you want dervishhood, spiritual poverty,
and emptiness, you must be friends with a sheikh.

Talking about it, reading books, and doing practices
don't help. Soul receives from soul that knowing.

The mystery of spiritual emptiness
may be living in a pilgrim's heart, and yet
the knowing of it may not yet be his.

Wait for the illuminating openness,
as though your chest were filling with light,
as when God said,

Did We not expand you?

(Qur'an 94:1)

Don't look for it outside yourself.
You are the source of milk. Don't milk others!

There is a milk fountain inside you.
Don't walk around with an empty bucket.

You have a channel into the ocean, and yet
you ask for water from a little pool.

Beg for that love expansion. Meditate only
on THAT. The Qur'an says,

And He is with you

(57:4).

There is a basket of fresh bread on your head,
and yet you go door to door asking for crusts.

Knock on your inner door. No other.
Sloshing knee-deep in fresh riverwater, yet
you keep wanting a drink from other people's waterbags.

Water is everywhere around you, but you see only
barriers that keep you from water.

The horse is beneath the rider's thighs, and still
he asks, "Where's my horse?"

Right there, under you!
"Yes, this is a horse, but where's the horse?"

Can't you see!
"Yes, I can see, but whoever saw such a horse?"

Mad with thirst, he can't drink from the stream
running so close by his face. He's like a pearl
on the deep bottom, wondering, inside his shell,
Where's the ocean?

His mental questionings
form the barrier. His physical eyesight
bandages his knowing. Self-consciousness
plugs his ears.

Stay bewildered in God,
and only that.

Those of you who are scattered,
simplify your worrying lives. There is *one*
righteousness: Water the fruit trees,
and don't water the thorns. Be generous
to what nurtures the spirit and God's luminous
reason-light. Don't honor what causes
dysentery and knotted-up tumors.

Don't feed both sides of yourself equally.
The spirit and the body carry different loads
and require different attentions.

Too often
we put saddlebags on Jesus and let the donkey
run loose in the pasture.

Don't make the body do
what the spirit does best, and don't put a big load
on the spirit that the body could carry easily.

WHEN WE PRAY ALONE

We are brought thick desserts, and we rarely refuse them.
We worship devoutly when we're with others.
Hours we sit, though we get up quickly

after a few minutes, when we pray alone.
We hurry down the gullet of our wantings.

But these qualities can change,
as minerals in the ground rise inside trees
and become tree, as a plant faces an animal
and enters the animal, so a human
can put down the heavy
body baggage and
be light.

ONE WHO WRAPS HIMSELF

God called the Prophet Muhammad *Muzzammil,*
"The One Who Wraps Himself,"
                              and said,
"Come out from under your cloak, you so fond
of hiding and running away.
                              Don't cover your face.
The world is a reeling, drunken body, and you
are its intelligent head.
                    Don't hide the candle
of your clarity. Stand up and burn
through the night, my prince.
                              Without your light
a great lion is held captive by a rabbit!

Be the captain of the ship,
Mustafa, my chosen one,
my expert guide.
                Look how the caravan of civilization
has been ambushed.
                    Fools are everywhere in charge.
Do not practice solitude like Jesus. Be *in*
the assembly,
                and take charge of it.
                                As the bearded griffin,
the *Humay,* lives on Mt. Qaf because he's native to it,
so you should live most naturally out in public
and be a communal teacher of souls."

A friend remarks to the Prophet, "Why is it
I get screwed in business deals?
It's like a spell. I become distracted
by business talk and make wrong decisions."

Muhammad replies, "Stipulate with every transaction
that you need three days to make sure."

Deliberation is one of the qualities of God.
Throw a dog a bit of something.
He sniffs to see if he wants it.

Be that careful.
Sniff with your wisdom-nose.
Get clear. Then decide.

The universe came into being gradually
over six days. God could have just commanded,
Be!
     Little by little a person reaches forty and fifty
and sixty, and feels more complete. God could have thrown
full-blown prophets flying through the cosmos in an instant.

Jesus said one word, and a dead man sat up,
but creation usually unfolds,
like calm breakers.

Constant, slow movement teaches us to keep working
like a small creek that stays clear,
that doesn't stagnate, but finds a way
through numerous details, deliberately.

Deliberation is born of joy,
like a bird from an egg.
                    Birds don't resemble eggs!
Think how different the hatching out is.

A white leathery snake egg, a sparrow's egg;
a quince seed, an apple seed: very different things
look similar at one stage.

These leaves, our bodily personalities, seem identical,
but the globe of soul fruit
we make,
each is elaborately
unique.

THE PRIVATE BANQUET

Muhammad, in the presence of Gabriel,

"Friend,
let me see you as you really are. Let me look
as an interested observer looks at his interest."

"You could not endure it. The sense of sight
is too weak to take in this reality."

"But show yourself
anyway, that I can understand what may not be known
with the senses."

The body senses are wavering and blurry,
but there is a clear fire inside,

a flame like Abraham,
that is Alpha and Omega. Human beings seem to be derived,
evolved, from this planet, but essentially,
humanity is the origin of the world.

Remember this!
A tiny gnat's outward form flies around and around
in pain and wanting, while the gnat's inward nature
includes the entire galactic whirling of the universe!

Muhammad persisted in his request,
and Gabriel revealed a single feather
that reached from the East to the West,
a glimpse that would have instantly crumbled
to powder a mountain range.

Muhammad stared, senseless.
Gabriel came and held him in his arms.

Awe serves
for strangers. This close-hugging love

is for friends.

Kings have formidable guards around them
with swords drawn, a public show of power
that keeps order and reduces arrogance and mischief
and other disasters.

But when the king comes
to the private banquet with his friends,
there's harp music and the flute.
No kettledrums.

And no keeping accounts,
no judging behavior, no helmets, no armor.

Just silk and music and beautiful women bringing cups.
You know how it is, but who can say it!

Conclude this part, my friend,
and lead us the way we should go.

✒

We are the night ocean filled
with glints of light. We are the space
between the fish and the moon,
while we sit here together.

✒

Which is worth more, a crowd of thousands,
or your own genuine solitude?
Freedom, or power over an entire nation?

A little while alone in your room
will prove more valuable than anything else
that could ever be given you.

1/24/98

25 ✦ Majesty:

This We Have Now

ON MAJESTY

One sufi image of the lines of transmission (silsila) *is a great branching rosebush that grows elegantly on many levels and within several worlds at once. Initiation and guidance come through the saints and keep the present moment dynamic and quivering with new growth. Majesty is that composite attention felt as a presence, dawn, a company of friends, a splendor that is prior to, and the source of, the universe. Rumi says it is a state of awareness best spoken of in terms of what it is* not.

THIS WE HAVE NOW

This we have now
is not imagination.

This is not
grief or joy.

Not a judging state,
or an elation,
or sadness.

Those come
and go.

This is the presence
that doesn't.

It's dawn, Husam,
here in the splendor of coral,
inside the Friend, the simple truth
of what Hallaj said.

What else could human beings want?

When grapes turn to wine,
they're wanting
this.

When the nightsky pours by,
it's really a crowd of beggars,
and they all want some of this!

This
that we are now
created the body, cell by cell,
like bees building a honeycomb.

The human body and the universe
grew from this, not this
from the universe and the human body.

THE VISIONS OF DAQUQI

Husam,
tell about the visions of Daquqi,
who said,
            "I have traveled East and West not knowing
which way I was going, following the moon,
lost inside God."
                  Someone asked, "Why do you go bare-
footed over the stones and thorns?"
                        "What," he answered.
"What."
        A bewildered lover doesn't walk on feet.
He or she walks on love. There are no "long"
or "short" trips for those. No time.

The body learned from the spirit how to travel.
A saint's body moves in the unconditioned way,
though it seems to be in conditionedness.

Daquqi said,
            "One day I was going along
looking to see in people the shining of the Friend,
so I would recognize the ocean in a drop,
the sun in a bright speck.
                        I came to the shore
at twilight and saw seven candles. I hurried
along the beach toward them. The light of each
lifted into the sky. I was amazed. My amazement
was amazed. Waves of bewilderment
broke over my head.

What are these candles that no one seems to see?
In the presence of such lights people were looking
for lamps to buy!
                  Then the seven became one,
in the middle of the sky's rim.
                              Then that
fanned out to seven again. There were connections
between the candles that cannot be said.
I saw, but I cannot say.

I ran closer. I fell. I lay there awhile.
I got up and ran again. I had no head and no feet.

They became seven men, and then seven trees,
so dense with leaves and fruit
that no limbs were visible.
                        Flashes of light
spurted from each fruit like juice!

And most marvelous of all was that hundreds
of thousands of people were passing beside the trees,
risking their lives, sacrificing everything,
to find some scrap of shade.
                              They made peculiar parasols
out of pieces of wool. They tried anything.

And no one saw the trees with their tremendous shade!
The caravans had no food, and yet food was dropping
all about them. If anyone had said,

       'Look! Over here!'
they would have thought him insane, or drunk.

How can this happen? Or am I dreaming?
I walk up to the trees. I eat the fruit.
I might as well believe.
     And still I see people
searching so desperately for an unripe grape,
with these vineyards around them,
heavy with perfect bunches.

Then the seven trees became one, and then seven again.
At every second they were both seven and one.

They were doing the ritual prayer, kneeling and bowing,
without knees or waists!
     Then they were seven men
seated in meditation for the sake of the one reality.

I came closer and waved. They called,
       'O Daquqi,
the glory and the crown!'
       'How do they know my name?'
I thought. 'They've never seen me till now.'

Immediately they knew my thought,
and smiled at each other.
      'Honored one,
is this still hidden from you? How can anything
be hidden from one so dissolved in God?'

'If this is the spirit-reality,' I said to myself,
'how is it we're speaking words and saying names?'

One of the seven answered, 'Names, sometimes
the names slip away, but it's not forgetfulness.
It's our being so absorbed.'

Then they all said to me,
'Would you lead us in prayer?'

'Yes. But wait awhile.
I am still in some temporal confusion
that will be solved by companionship with you.

Through companionship with the ground a grapevine
grows. It opens into the earth's darkness
and flies. It becomes selfless
in the presence of its origin and learns
what it really is.'
They nodded, as though saying,
'Whenever you're ready.' That nodding
was a flame in my heart.
I was freed from hourly time,
from sequence and relation."

Everyone has a stable
and a trainer appointed to him or her. If you break away,
the trainer comes and gets you. You think
you're making choices, but the trainer is actually
leading you around.
You like to deny
that you have a keeper. You say,
"It's my powerful
animal urges."

THE WORM'S WAKING

This is how a human being can change:

there's a worm addicted to eating
grape leaves.
Suddenly, he wakes up,

Whoa!

call it grace, whatever, something
wakes him, and he's no longer
a worm.
He's the entire vineyard,
and the orchard too, the fruit, the trunks,
a growing wisdom and joy
that doesn't need
to devour.

THE FRESHNESS

When it's cold and raining,
you are more beautiful.

And the snow brings me
even closer to your lips.

The inner secret, that which was never born,
you are that freshness, and I am with you now.

I can't explain the goings,
or the comings. You enter suddenly,

and I am nowhere again.
Inside the majesty.

JUDGE A MOTH BY THE BEAUTY OF ITS CANDLE

You are the king's son.
Why do you close yourself up?
Become a lover.

Don't aspire to be a general
or a minister of state.

One is a boredom for you,
the other a disgrace.

You've been a picture on a bathhouse wall
long enough. No one recognizes you here, do they?

God's lion disguised as a human being!
I saw that and put down the book
I was studying, Hariri's *Maqamat*.

There is no early and late for us.
The only way to measure a lover
is by the grandeur of the beloved.

Judge a moth by the beauty of its candle.

Shams is invisible because he is inside sight.
He is the intelligent essence
of what is everywhere at once, seeing.

The morning wind spreads its fresh smell.
We must get up and take that in,
that wind that lets us live.
Breathe before it's gone.

Slave, be aware that the Lord
of all the East is here.

A flickering storm cloud
shows his lightnings to you!

Your words are guesswork.
He speaks from experience.
There's a huge difference.

26 ~ Evolutionary Intelligence: Say I Am You

ON EVOLVING

The movement from mineral to plant to animal to human and beyond is often mentioned in Rumi's poetry. The successive "deaths" that are gone through as the soul ascends returning to God do not involve a severing from a lower form and a release into a higher. Rather, each stage is incorporated in the next. In this section the pronouns widen out to the most inclusive model for identity I know of, from Jelaluddin to the surf and the evening breeze and the nightsky to the ultimate you. This progression cannot be spoken, and yet Rumi calls into the cosmos, "Say I am you." He so obviously loves the world and each disguise the spirit takes. He savors the taste of being dust grain, chickpea, dog, camel, poet. This enthusiasm and joy in the moving through is primary, and it is difficult for some Westerners to accept. Tragic knowledge, grief, life as gradual subtraction—these are not the core insights for Rumi. At the center is a clarity, a great generous laughter, and love that sees how everything alchemizes into the Friend. Some essential companionship flows as the lifeblood in Rumi's divine comedy.

A DOVE IN THE EAVES

When I press my hand to my chest,
it is your chest.

And now you're scratching my head!

Sometimes you put me in the herd
with your other camels.

Sometimes you place me at the front of the troops
as the commander. Sometimes you wet me
with your mouth like you do your seal-ring
just before you plant your power.

Sometimes you round me
into a simple door knocker.

You take blood and make sperm.
You take sperm and create an animal.
You use the animal to evolve intelligence.
Life keeps leading to more life.

You drive me away gently
as a flute song does a dove
from the eaves.

With the same song
you call me back.

You push me out on many journeys;
then you anchor me with no motion at all.

I am water. I am the thorn
that catches someone's clothing.

I don't care about marvelous sights!
I only want to be in your presence.

There's nothing to *believe*.
Only when I quit believing in myself
did I come into this beauty.

I saw your blade and burned my shield!
I flew on six hundred pairs of wings like Gabriel.
But now that I'm here, what do I need wings for?

Day and night I guarded the pearl of my soul.
Now in this ocean of pearling currents,
I've lost track of which was mine.

There is no way to describe you.
Say the end of this so strongly
that I will ride up over
my own commotion.

꙳

We have this way of talking, and we have another.
Apart from what we wish and what we fear may happen,

we are alive with other life, as clear stones
take form in the mountain.

꙳

This piece of food cannot be eaten,
nor this bit of wisdom found by looking.
There is a secret core in everyone not
even Gabriel can know by trying to know.

꙳

In the slaughterhouse of love, they kill
only the best, none of the weak or deformed.
Don't run away from this dying.
Whoever's not killed for love is dead meat.

꙳

THE WITNESS, THE DARLING

Muhammad could mediate
for every kind of disgrace,
because he looked so unswervingly
at God. His eye medicine came
from his ever-expanding into God.

Any orphan daubed with that salve
will get better. He could see all
the attainments of those on the way.

Hence God called him "the witness."

The tools of the witness are truthfulness
and keen seeing and the night vigil.

"Deep Feelings, Deep-Witnessing"

This is the witness a judge listens
most carefully to. A false witness
has some self-interest that makes
his testimony specious.

He can't see the whole. That's why God
wants you to deny your desires, so
you will learn how to give up self-interest.

It's the love of the manifest world
that makes you an unreliable witness.

There is another way of seeing
that sees *through* your love of this place,
through the exciting drunkenness to the headache.
The witness can cure that hurting.

God is the just judge,
who calls the true witness,
the eye of pure love,
the darling,
              the dalliance,
the reason inside the playfulness
that created phenomena.

IN THE ARC OF YOUR MALLET

Don't go anywhere without me.
Let nothing happen in the sky apart from me,
or on the ground, in this world or that world,
without my being in its happening.
Vision, see nothing I don't see.
Language, say nothing.
The way the night knows itself with the moon,
be that with me. Be the rose
nearest to the thorn that I am.

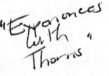
"Experiences with Thorns"

"Experiences Next to the Well — Tub Springs"

271

I want to feel myself in you when you taste food,
in the arc of your mallet when you work,
when you visit friends, when you go
up on the roof by yourself at night.

There's nothing worse than to walk out along the street
without you. I don't know where I'm going.
You're the road and the knower of roads,
more than maps, more than love.

UNMARKED BOXES

Don't grieve. Anything you lose comes round
in another form. The child weaned from mother's milk
now drinks wine and honey mixed.

God's joy moves from unmarked box to unmarked box,
from cell to cell. As rainwater, down into flowerbed.
As roses, up from ground.
Now it looks like a plate of rice and fish,
now a cliff covered with vines,
now a horse being saddled.
It hides within these,
till one day it cracks them open.

Part of the self leaves the body when we sleep
and changes shape. You might say, "Last night
I was a cypress tree, a small bed of tulips,
a field of grapevines." Then the phantasm goes away.
You're back in the room.
I don't want to make anyone fearful.
Hear what's behind what I say.

Tatatumtum tatum tatadum.
There's the light gold of wheat in the sun
and the gold of bread made from that wheat.
I have neither. I'm only talking about them,

as a town in the desert looks up
at stars on a clear night.

THE MILK OF MILLENNIA

I am part of the load
not rightly balanced.
I drop off in the grass,
like the old cave-sleepers, to browse
wherever I fall.

For hundreds of thousands of years I have been dust grains
floating and flying in the will of the air,
often forgetting ever being
in that state, but in sleep
I migrate back. I spring loose
from the four-branched, time-and-space cross,
this waiting room.

I walk into a huge pasture.
I nurse the milk of millennia.

Everyone does this in different ways.
Knowing that conscious decisions
and personal memory
are much too small a place to live,
every human being streams at night
into the loving nowhere, or during the day,
in some absorbing work.

THE *YOU* PRONOUN

In the Name of God, the Merciful and Compassionate.
The start of the second book of the *Mathnawi* has been postponed,
and the reason is this: sometimes God reveals *all* the wisdom of doing
a certain action, and the listener becomes so overwhelmed in contem-
plating that, that he is unable to perform it. Lost in the infinity, with
no ability to understand, or *do*, anything.
God then reduces the wisdom portion, and makes a small bridle to
fit over the listener's head to lead him by. The size of the bridle is im-
portant when you're dealing with a stubborn camel. Too heavy, and
he'll lie down and refuse to move. Too slight, and he'll ignore it. The
proportion of wisdom to personal advantage is a subtle mixture, like

that of clay and water to make bricks. Too little water, and it won't cohere. Too much, and it washes away. God gives attention to an individual's balance, except when giving to those described in the text, *He gives, and they receive without calculating.* But that state cannot be understood without tasting it.

Someone once asked, "What is love?"

"Be lost in me," I said. "You'll know love when that happens."

Love has no calculating in it. That's why it's said to be a quality of God and not of human beings. "God loves you" is the only possible sentence. The subject becomes the object so totally that it can't be turned around. Who will the "you" pronoun stand for, if you say, "You love God"?

Prose Preface to Book II

BIRDSONG FROM INSIDE THE EGG

Sometimes a lover of God may faint
in the presence. Then the beloved bends
and whispers in his ear, "Beggar, spread out
your robe. I'll fill it with gold.

I've come to protect your consciousness.
Where has it gone? Come back into awareness!"

This fainting is because
lovers want *so much*.

A chicken invites a camel into her henhouse,
and the whole structure is demolished.

A rabbit nestles down
with its eyes closed
in the arms of a lion.

There is an *excess*
in spiritual searching
that is profound ignorance.

Let that ignorance be our teacher!
The Friend breathes into one
who has no breath.

A deep silence revives the listening
and the speaking of those two
who meet on the riverbank.

Like the ground turning green in a spring wind.
Like birdsong beginning inside the egg.

Like this universe coming into existence,
the lover wakes, and whirls
in a dancing joy,

then kneels down
in praise.

— Wow!

SAY I AM YOU

I am dust particles in sunlight.
I am the round sun.

To the bits of dust I say, *Stay*.
To the sun, *Keep moving*.

I am morning mist,
and the breathing of evening.

I am wind in the top of a grove,
and surf on the cliff.

Mast, rudder, helmsman, and keel,
I am also the coral reef they founder on.

I am a tree with a trained parrot in its branches.
Silence, thought, and voice.

The musical air coming through a flute,
a spark of a stone, a flickering

in metal. Both candle,
and the moth crazy around it.

Rose, and the nightingale
lost in the fragrance.

I am all orders of being, the circling galaxy,
the evolutionary intelligence, the lift,

and the falling away. What is,
and what isn't. You who know

Jelaluddin, You the one
in all, say who

I am. Say I
am You.

27 ✧ The Turn:

Dance in Your Blood

ON THE TURN

The "turn," the moving meditation done by Mevlevi dervishes, originated with Rumi. The story goes that he was walking in the goldsmithing section of Konya when he heard a beautiful music in their hammering. He began turning in harmony with it, an ecstatic dance of surrender and yet with great centered discipline. He arrived at a place where ego dissolves and a resonance with universal soul comes in. Dervish literally means "doorway." When what is communicated moves from presence to presence, darshan occurs, with language inside the seeing. When the gravitational pull gets even stronger, the two become one turning that is molecular and galactic and a spiritual remembering of the presence at the center of the universe. Turning is an image of how the dervish becomes an empty place where human and divine can meet. To approach the whole the part must become mad, by conventional standards at least. These ecstatic holy people, called matzubs in the sufi tradition, redefine this sort of madness as true health.

When he saw the dervishes in Cairo in 1910, Rainer Maria Rilke, the great spiritual poet of this century, said the turn was a form of kneeling. "It is so truly the mystery of the kneeling of the deeply kneeling man. With Rumi the scale is shifted, for in following the peculiar weight and strength in his knees, he belongs to that world in which height is depth. This is the night of radiant depth unfolded." December 17 is celebrated each year as Rumi's Wedding Night, the night he died in 1273 and reached full union.

Inside water, a waterwheel turns.
A star circulates with the moon.

We live in the night ocean wondering,
What are these lights?

៚

You have said what you are.
I am what I am.
Your actions in my head,
my head here in my hands
with something circling inside.
I have no name
for what circles
so perfectly.

៚

A secret turning in us
makes the universe turn.
Head unaware of feet,
and feet head. Neither cares.
They keep turning.

៚

This moment this love comes to rest in me,
many beings in one being.
In one wheat grain a thousand sheaf stacks.
Inside the needle's eye a turning night of stars.

៚

Keep walking, though there's no place to get to.
Don't try to see through the distances.
That's not for human beings. Move within,
but don't move the way fear makes you move.

៚

Walk to the well.
Turn as the earth and the moon turn,
circling what they love.
Whatever circles comes from the center.

❧

I circle your nest tonight,
around and around until morning
when a breath of air says, *Now,*
and the Friend holds up like a goblet
some anonymous skull.

❧

No better love than love with no object,
no more satisfying work than work with no purpose.

If you could give up tricks and cleverness,
that would be the cleverest trick!

❧

Some nights stay up till dawn,
as the moon sometimes does for the sun.
Be a full bucket pulled up the dark way
of a well, then lifted out into light.

❧

I am so small I can barely be seen.
How can this great love be inside me?

Look at your eyes. They are small,
but they see enormous things.

❧

When you feel your lips becoming infinite
and sweet, like the moon in a sky,
when you feel that spaciousness inside,
Shams of Tabriz will be there too.

❧

The sun is love. The lover,
a speck circling the sun.

A Spring wind moves to dance
any branch that isn't dead.

❧

Something opens our wings. Something
makes boredom and hurt disappear.
Someone fills the cup in front of us.
We taste only sacredness.

❧

Held like this, to draw in milk,
no will, tasting clouds of milk,
never so content.

❧

I stand up, and this one of me
turns into a hundred of me.
They say I circle around you.
Nonsense. I circle around me.

❧

I have lived on the lip
of insanity, wanting to know reasons,
knocking on a door. It opens.
I've been knocking from the inside!

❧

Real value comes with madness,
matzub below, scientist above.

Whoever finds love
beneath hurt and grief

disappears into emptiness
with a thousand new disguises.

❧

Dance, when you're broken open.
Dance, if you've torn the bandage off.
Dance in the middle of the fighting.
Dance in your blood.
Dance, when you're perfectly free.

✍ Notes

ON RUMI

Fariddin Attar (1119–1230) was the great perfumist and physician-poet, author of *The Conference of the Birds*. He is said to have met Rumi in Damascus when Rumi was a boy of twelve traveling with his father. Attar immediately recognized Rumi's spiritual eminence. He saw the father walking ahead of the son and said, "Here comes a sea followed by an ocean." He gave the boy his *Asranama,* a book about the entanglement of the soul in the material world.

Annemarie Schimmel has been immersed in Rumi for over forty years. Her scholarship and devotion are magnificent. *The Triumphal Sun: A Study of the Works of Jalaloddin Rumi* (1978) and *I Am Wind, You Are Fire: The Life and Work of Rumi* (1992) are classics in the field.

A NOTE ON THE ORGANIZATION OF THIS BOOK

Alast is the primordial covenant that occurs when God addresses the not-yet-created humanity, "Am I not your lord? *Alastu bi-rabbikum.*" Rumi hears the question as a creative music that makes all creatures come forth in a loving dance of reply, "Yes!"

CHAPTER 1. THE TAVERN

On the tavern: Nasruddin is a Middle Eastern trickster figure.

"A Children's Game" Hakim Sanai (d. 1131), the eloquent court poet of Ghazna, was the first to use the *mathnawi* form, rhyming couplets expressing mystical and didactic themes. Rumi borrows many images and phrases and stories from Sanai, particularly from his *Hadiqat al-haqiqa, The Orchard of Truth*. Sanai's earthy style impressed Rumi. His remark that dirty jokes can be instructional finds its way into Book V of the *Mathnawi,* where a number of such jokes are told and explicated. Sanai is also the source of the famous story of the blind man and the elephant, which Rumi changes to a number of people in a darkened room trying to describe an elephant by where they happen to touch it (p. 252). Sanai got the story from Indian sources. The tricky pun *bargi bi bargi* (the leaves of leaflessness) also comes from Sanai. Rumi uses the image of "no-leaves" blooming on a winter tree as a beautiful symbol for the state of awareness that has abandoned the world without leaving (!) it.

Hu is the pronoun of divine presence.

"Special Plates": The word *Shams* means "the sun," and almost every use of sunlight in Rumi's poetry is a remembrance of Shams of Tabriz, the wandering mystic whom Rumi met in 1244, when he was thirty-seven. Shams was fifty, perhaps sixty. Their Friendship is one of the central icons of mysticism. They merged in a duet of being that became a single note. Teacher and student, lover and beloved, existence and non-existence, light and the source of light, presence and absence, all distinctions dissolved in the mystical conversation (*sohbet*) that they became. Rumi's son, Sultan Velad, writes that Shams passed through all the lower stages of enthusiastic lovers of God and became *qotb-e hama ma shugan,* the pole of the beloved. When he arrived in 1244 in the vicinity of Konya, he was an overwhelming spiritual presence, a wild sun-lion, who avoided the society of the learned, especially theologians. He stayed on the outskirts in a caravanserai, home for the homeless and wanderers. One version of the meeting of Rumi and Shams says that their first encounter occurred in the caravanserai of the sugar merchants. Husam Chelebi, Rumi's scribe, was a student of Shams. He also is closely associated with sunlight, "the radiance of truth, Husamuddin."

Rumi scholar Annemarie Schimmel provides what facts are known about Shams in her *The Triumphal Sun: A Study of the Works of Jalaloddin Rumi* (London: East-West Publications, 1978), 16–25. Aflaki, a fourteenth-century writer and friend of Rumi's grandson, gives the more legendary version.

CHAPTER 2. BEWILDERMENT

"I Have Five Things to Say": Rabia (d. 801), the great woman mystic from Basra, said that God should be loved not out of fear or hope, but for his beauty, and that that beauty is in the heart. She once sat indoors on a lovely Spring day to teach that external magnificence is only a reflection of God's inner kindness and generosity.

The *sema* is the ecstatic dance of turning.

"Saladin's Begging Bowl": Saladin refers to Saladin Zarkub, the goldsmith, the Friend Rumi found after Shams disappeared. There are hagiographic miniatures that show Rumi leading Saladin out of his goldsmith's shop and onto the street to begin the *sema;* Rumi had heard a transcendent music in the goldsmith's hammering. Saladin had come to Konya in 1235, already a student, like Rumi, of Burhan Mahaqqiq. It is said that when Shams arrived, the two (Rumi and Shams) often met in Saladin's shop or in his home. Sometime after Shams's disappearance Saladin became the company that Rumi needed, the reminder of deep presence. Saladin, in a different way from Shams, was also a problem for Rumi's disciples. He was uneducated, almost illiterate. While Shams was a profound student of scripture, Saladin could not recite the first sura of the Qur'an correctly! Rumi, though, recognized him as his next guide.

He that came last year in red [Shams]
appears now in a brown robe [Saladin].

The Friendship was further bonded by the marriage of Rumi's son, Sultan Velad, to Saladin's daughter. Several of Rumi's letters are addressed to the young couple. A number of poems end with Saladin's name in the author's place of honor. In 1258 when Saladin died, Rumi led a glorious mystical dance with flute and drum through the streets of Konya to celebrate the *urs,* the spiritual wedding of a great saint.

"Where Are We?" In Persian the imagery of the last stanza contains a complex pun. *Maku* means "a weaver's shuttle." *Ma ku* means "Where are we?" Rumi often uses elaborate puns that are almost impossible to translate.

CHAPTER 3. EMPTINESS AND SILENCE

"The Reed Flute's Song": The poem is in the *mathnawi* (rhyming couplet) form. One day Husam and Rumi were walking in the gardens of Meram. Husam suggested that Rumi begin a poem in the *mathnawi* form, whereupon Rumi pulled the first eighteen lines of "The Reed Flute's Song," which he had already written down, out of his turban. The deep, synchronistic, collaborative coupleting had already begun! Annemarie Schimmel has a beautiful image for what the six books of the *Mathnawi* became during the next twelve years of Rumi and Husam's collaboration. She likens it to a *medrese,* a dervish learning community, and in particular, the Qaratay center in Konya, which was built a few years before the *Mathnawi* was begun. The walls and the ceiling inside are covered with exquisite knotted Kufic script, very complicated so that only the initiated can decipher it. The design as a whole leads the attention upward to a dome, where the inlays change to a star pattern. "The eye wanders finding no beginning or end," until it reaches the apex, which is open, and through which at night stars are seen and reflected in a tiny pond in the center of the floor. The ineffable density, woven, rising out of a Qur'anic base, boundaryless yet centered in a starry, small-pond transparency—this is how the *Mathnawi* feels. The Qaratay meeting room, which can still be visited in Konya, makes a fine metaphor. All of Rumi's poetry is discourse with and within a community, *sohbet,* the mystical companionship beyond the limits of time and space.

"Sanai": *Rum* equals *Rome,* a designation for the western half of Anatolia, which was formerly a part of the Roman Empire. This is the source of Rumi's name, "the one from Roman Anatolia." In dialectical Arabic to this day, the adjective *rumi* refers to that which is Western or nonindigenous.

"No Flag": Azar was Abraham's father and a famous image maker. In the Qur'an Abraham asks his father, "Do you take idols for gods?"

CHAPTER 4. SPRING GIDDINESS

"Unfold Your Own Myth": The line "Chase a deer and end up everywhere!" is a reference to Ibrahim (d. 783), whose story is given below. A prince of Balkh, Ibrahim represents to the sufis someone who in one visionary moment gives up his external kingdom for the inner majesty. There are striking similarities between his life and Gautama the Buddha's. Balkh seems to have been an area where Buddhism, Islam, and Christianity met and blended; lotus motifs appear on the ancient ruins there. Here is Rumi's account of Ibrahim's epiphany:

> Ibrahim, when he was still king, went out hunting. As he galloped after a deer, he became separated from his retinue. His horse was tired and lathered, but still Ibrahim rode. Deep in the wilderness, the fleeing deer turned its head and spoke, "You were not created for this chase. This deer body did not take shape out of nothingness, so that you might hunt. Supposing you catch me, will that be enough?" Ibrahim heard these words deeply and cried out. He reined in his horse and dismounted. There was a shepherd nearby. "Take this royal jacket sewn with jewels. Take my horse and my bow. Give me your shepherd's robe of coarse cloth, and tell no one what has happened!" The exchange was made, and Ibrahim set out on his new life. He made such an extraordinary effort to catch the deer and ended up being caught by God! All plans are subject to revision. God lives between a human being and the object of his or her desire. "It's all a mystical journey to the Friend." (Discourse #44)

CHAPTER 7. SOHBET

"In Between Stories": Husam Chelebi was the scribe to whom Rumi dictated the entire Mathnawi, but he was also much more than a secretary. Rumi said that Husam was the source of the words. Rumi claimed only to be the flute. Husam was the flute player and the breath, the Mathnawi itself being the song. Husam was a student of Shams. It is through him, then, that the voice of the beloved is made audible. Rumi says that Husam belongs to that class of saints who are not content with silent contemplation but who must express their knowing.

CHAPTER 9. THE PICKAXE

"Zikr": Zikr (or dhikr) means remembrance. In a practical sense it refers to the internal or external repetition of the phrase La'illaha il'Allahu ("there is no reality but God; there is only God"). The zikr is said to have at least three parts. The first part, La'illaha, is the denial, the abandonment of everything, the depths. The second part, il'Allah, is the actual intrusion, the explosion into the individual, of divine presence. Hu, the third part, is the out-breathing of that divine presence.

One sufi teacher, Bawa Muhaiyaddeen, advised his students to repeat and reflect upon the *zikr* with every breath. A student asked the teacher, "But how is that possible—I mean, how could anyone *do* that?" The teacher said, "It is like driving a car. At first you think it is difficult, but you get used to it. It becomes natural. After awhile, you can even drive and talk at the same time."

CHAPTER 10. ART AS FLIRTATION WITH SURRENDER

"Omar and the Old Poet": Omar (d. 644) was the second caliph, designated as such by Abu Bakr on his deathbed. Omar is famous for his strong will and his direct, impetuous character. He formed the Islamic state and expanded it into Syria, Iraq, Egypt, and Libya.

CHAPTER 11. UNION

"Ayaz and the King's Pearl": Ayaz is the servant who is completely obedient to his master, King Mahmud (which means "Praise to the end!"). This love between king and slave as an image of that between lover and beloved is a story retold in many mystical sources (Ghazzali, Attar, Sanai). Rumi's version adds a striking new touch. Ayaz goes to a secret closet every morning. The courtiers suspect he's hiding something, but the "treasure" turns out to be only an old sheepskin jacket and Ayaz's worn-out work shoes. He goes there to meditate on them as reminders of his state before he was called to the king's service. Rumi says that to remember who one was before the advent of grace is to know one's lord.

CHAPTER 14. THE HOWLING NECESSITY

"Love Dogs": *Khidr* means, literally, "the green one." Khidr is known throughout the Islamic world. He exists on the edge between the seen and the unseen. When Moses vows to find the place "where the two seas meet," meaning where the spiritual and the worldly mix, he meets Khidr. Although not mentioned by name in the Qur'an, Khidr is associated with the person described as "one of our servants whom We [God] had given mercy from Us, and We had taught him knowledge proceeding from Us" (Qur'an 18:64, Arberry translation).

In this passage, Moses wants to follow Khidr and learn from him, but Khidr says, "If you follow me, you must not question anything I do. You must be patient and wait for my explanations." Moses agrees, but as Khidr performs apparent outrages (sinking a boat, killing a boy), Moses cannot restrain his alarm, and Khidr leaves him after explaining the hidden reasons for his actions. Khidr represents the inner dimension, which transcends form. He is the personification of the revealing function of the metaphysical intellect, the "prophetic soul." He especially appears to solitaries, those who are cut off from normal channels of spiritual instruction. The sufi mystic Ibrahim, who gave up his external kingdom for the kingdom within, said this of Khidr: "I lived four years in the wilderness. Khidr the Green Ancient was my companion. He taught me the Great Name of God."

Khidr is connected philologically with Elijah and with Utnapishtim of the Gilgamesh epic. He may be a partial source, along with Druidic lore, for the enigmatic Green Knight in the Middle English poem "Sir Gawain and the Green Knight."

CHAPTER 20. IN BAGHDAD, DREAMING OF CAIRO

"Human Honesty": Bayazid Bestami (d. 877) wrote nothing, but many of his ecstatic sayings have been preserved:

> "How great is my glory!"
> "I am the wine drinker and the wine and the cupbearer."
> "I came forth from Bayazid-ness as a snake from its skin."
> "Then I looked and saw that lover and beloved are one."
> "I was the smith of my own self."
> "I am the throne and the footstool."
> "Your obedience to me is greater than my obedience to You."
> "I am the well-preserved tablet."
> "I saw the Kaaba walking around me!"

Bestami illustrates the state of *fana,* of being so dissolved in God that what is said is said by the divine presence. In meditation Bestami developed an extremely daring sense of the numinous. His mystical experiences transcended any distinctions between subject and object, and/or any qualities attributed to either. His utterances have been preserved and treasured in sufi circles for a thousand years. In Rumi's work he is often mentioned in balance with Junnaiyd, who advocated spiritual sobriety as much as Bestami did spiritual drunkenness. Junnaiyd said, "There is a sobriety that contains all drunkennesses, but there is no drunkenness that contains all sobriety."

Bestami's teacher in this way of mystical union was Abu Ali al-Sindi, who knew no Arabic. Bestami had to teach his teacher enough Arabic to say the prayers from the Qur'an. In return, al-Sindi led Bestami deep into the path of meditation. Perhaps it could be said that in Bestami we find the blending of Islamic and Indian mysticisms into an unnameable, and wholly original, stream.

"Sheikh Kharraqani": Sheikh Kharraqani (Abu'l-Hasan Kharraqani) was a model of one who endures with patience and so masters the lower energies (*nafs*) that he can be depicted riding a lion, using a snake for a riding crop!

Qutb means "axis," "pole," "the center," which contains the periphery or is present in it. The *qutb* is a spiritual being, or function, which can reside in a human being or several human beings or a moment. It is the elusive mystery of how the divine gets delegated into the manifest world and obviously cannot be defined.

"Ali in Battle": Ali (598–661) was Muhammad's cousin, also his son-in-law and the Fourth Caliph. Ali's tomb is in Najaf, Iraq. He was one of the first converts to Islam. Ali's relationship with Muhammad was a special one. Twice he's referred to in the Qur'an as "my brother" and three times as "my heir." Muhammad blessed the marriage of his daughter Fatima and Ali by anointing them on their wedding night. Anointing is not a feature of Islamic ritual, and, as far as is known, Muhammad did this for no one else. Ali is recognized by sufi mystics as a fountainhead of the esoteric secrets, and more generally he is remembered as a model of *futuwwah* (or chivalry), as a great warrior, and for his learning. It was Ali who first laid down the rules of formal Arabic grammar, notably describing language as made up of nouns, verbs, and particles. The sayings and sermons of Ali are collected in *The Way of Eloquence,* which serves as a model for Arabic usage, much as the orations of Cicero did, until very recently, in the West.

CHAPTER 24. WISHED-FOR SONG

On Secrecy: *Chilla* is a forty-day period of seclusion and meditation and fasting. Rumi kept many of these, sometimes three in a row, under the tutelage of Burhan Mahaqqiq. *Qibla* is the point of the prayer rug, hence the direction of a person's prayers.

"One Who Wraps Himself": The humay is a legendary bird whose shadow is said to confer kinship. Mt. Qaf (abundance) is the mountain at the end of the world near the divine where, in Rumi's mythology, the humay lives.

CHAPTER 25. MAJESTY

"This We Have Now": All of Rumi's poetry comes from work within a community. In this particular segment the group has stayed up on an all-night vigil, so that the dawn itself becomes an image of the state of awareness all have reached, which is called splendor and friendship and "the truth that Hallaj spoke." Al-Hallaj Mansour is the sufi mystic martyred in Baghdad in 922 for saying *Ana'l-Haqq* or "I am the truth" or "I am God." The ineffable inner majesty celebrated here is prior to the existence of the universe and the seed that it grew from.

"The Visions of Daquqi": Daquqi's vision of the seven candles becoming one may refer to the oneness of the prophets, the essential core of all religions, or it may refer to the unity of the seven principal divine names (living, *hayy;* knowing, *alim;* willing, *murid;* mighty, *adir;* hearing, *sami;* seeing, *basir;* and speaking, *mutakallim*); or it may refer to other mysteries.

"Judge a Moth": Hariri's *Maqamat* was a famous rhetoric text of the time, which classified the forms of artistic expression.

✺ A Note on These Translations and a Few Recipes

[handwritten annotations: "8/5/98", "The Spaciousness + longing in Rumi's Poetry"]

My academic training, at Berkeley and Chapel Hill, was in American and twentieth-century literature. I had never even heard Rumi's name until 1976, when Robert Bly handed me a copy of A. J. Arberry's translations, saying, "These poems need to be released from their cages." How any translator chooses to work on one poet, and not on others, is a mysterious thing. Some attunement must be there. I felt drawn immediately to the spaciousness and longing in Rumi's poetry. I began to explore this new world, rephrasing Arberry's English. I sent some of the early attempts to a friend who was teaching law at Rutgers-Camden. He, inexplicably, read them to his class. A young law student came up afterward, asked him for my address, and started writing, urging me to come meet his teacher in Philadelphia. When I finally did walk into the room where the Sri Lankan saint Bawa Muhaiyaddeen sat on his bed talking to a small group, I realized that I had met this man in a dream the year before. I can't explain such an event, nor can I deny that it did happen. Bawa told me to continue with the Rumi work; "It has to be done." But, he cautioned, "If you work on the words of a *gnani*, you must become a *gnani*," a master. I did not become one of those, but for nine years, for four or five intervals during each year, I was in the presence of one.

Rumi says,

> Mind does its fine-tuning hair-splitting,
> but no craft or art begins
> or can continue without a master
> giving wisdom into it.

I would have little notion of what Rumi's poetry is about or what it came out of if I were not connected to this sufi sheikh. Though it's not necessary to use the word *sufi*. The work Bawa did and does with me is beyond religion. "Love is the religion, and the universe is the book." Working on Rumi's poetry deepens the inner companionship. My apprenticeship continues, and whatever else they are, these versions or translations or renderings or imitations are homage to a teacher. And yet not as a follower, more as a friend. In some way I am very grateful for, these poems feel as if they come as part of a continuing conversation rather than as language unilaterally produced. I once asked Bawa if what I saw in his eyes could someday come up behind my eyes and look out. He began to talk about the subtle relationship between a teacher and the community, "Not until the *I* becomes *we*."

There was a childhood joke that I did not get until recently. At age six I was a geography freak. I memorized all the capitals of all the countries in the 1943 *Rand McNally Atlas*. I grew up on the campus of a boys' school in Chattanooga, and the teachers were continually testing this odd expertise. "Bulgaria!" someone would call out across the quadrangle. "Sophia!" I would answer. I couldn't be stumped, until the ecstatic trickster, James Pennington, went down in his basement Latin classroom and came up with a country that had no capital, on his map at least: Cappadocia. The look on my face, what I *didn't* know, named me. From then on I was called "Cappadocia," or "Capp." I almost fell down a few years ago when I remembered the nickname and realized that the central city of that Anatolian area was Iconium, now Konya, where Rumi lived and is buried. *Rumi* means "the one from Roman Anatolia." I don't mean to claim a special relationship with Rumi. Mevlana's poetry has been a large part of my life for twenty years. It has brought many friends and wonderful opportunities. But a poet of such astonishing range and depth needs many translators and interpreters. Mystical poetry tries to reveal the apple orchard *within* the mist of language (Rumi's image). I hope these translations do not thicken that fog; I hope they burn it off! I do love the apples that Rumi loves. The synchronicities that introduced us continue to delight and exfoliate in wonderful ways. This work has involved a kind of emptying out, a surrender (despite the strutting of personal incidents here). That's how the collaboration has felt. It's also a form of healing, a way to play and praise, and an unfolding friendship with a teacher. Or just say that all these poems are love poems. Of course, they are, self to deep self, plural to singular, Coleman to Bawa, Rumi to Shams, I to you, Lover-beloved-love, ecstatic universes in synchrony. Rumi is God's funny family on a big open radio line.

On the more literal level, the texts I work from to produce these poems are unpublished translations done by John Moyne, Emeritus Head of Linguistics at the City University of New York, and the following translations by Reynold Nicholson and A. J. Arberry, the famous Cambridge Islamicists:

The Mathnawi of Jalaluddin Rumi. Translated by Reynold Nicholson. 8 vols. London: Luzac, 1925–1940.
Mystical Poems of Rumi. Translated by A. J. Arberry. Persian Heritage Series, no. 3. Chicago: Univ. of Chicago Press, 1968.
Mystical Poems of Rumi. Translated by A. J. Arberry. Persian Heritage Series, no. 23. Boulder, CO: Westview Press, 1979.
The Rubaiyat of Jalal al-din Rumi: Select Translations into English Verse. Translated by A. J. Arberry. London: Emery Walker, 1949.

John Moyne and I try to be faithful to the images, the tone as we hear it, and the spiritual information coming through. We have not tried to reproduce any of the dense musicality of the Persian originals. It has seemed appropriate to place Rumi in the strong tradition of American free verse, which has the inner searching, the delicacy, and the simple groundedness that also characterize Rumi's poetry. These are free translations, but I hope they remain true to the essence.

A FEW RECIPES

Rumi often speaks of the relationship between teacher and student as that between the cook and the chickpea in the pot. "You think I'm torturing you. I'm giving you flavor, so you can mix with rice and spices and be the lovely vitality of a human being." Here is a recipe for chickpeas from Kashmir.

CHANA MASALEDAR

> 4 tablespoons vegetable oil
> 1 teaspoon whole cumin seeds
> 1 medium onion, peeled and chopped
> 1/2 teaspoon ground cinnamon
> 1/2 teaspoon ground nutmeg
> 1/2 teaspoon ground cloves

1/2 teaspoon ground coriander
3 cloves garlic, peeled and minced
a piece of fresh ginger, about 1/2 inch square, peeled and grated
2 tablespoons tomato paste
24-ounce can of chickpeas (garbanzos)
salt to taste
1/2 teaspoon cayenne pepper
2 tablespoons lemon juice

Garnish

3 tomatoes, quartered
1 medium onion
4 green chilies, or a green pepper sliced

Heat the oil in a large heavy skillet. When hot, put in the whole cumin seeds. As soon as they begin to darken, after a few seconds, put in the chopped onion. Stir and fry for 7 minutes. Turn heat to low and add the cinnamon, nutmeg, cloves, and coriander. Mix and add the garlic and ginger, stirring for 3 minutes. Add the tomato paste. Open chickpeas and drain out most of the liquid, leaving a couple of tablespoons. Pour this and the chickpeas into the skillet. Add salt, cayenne, and lemon juice. Mix well, cover, and let the flavors combine for about 10 minutes. Stir gently every now and then, taking care not to break the chickpeas. Serve with basmati rice in a bowl lined with quartered tomatoes, raw onion slivers, and either green chilies or slices of green pepper. Serves 4.

EARLY MORNING CURRY

1 large onion: chop small
2 chili peppers: chop small
1 small cabbage: chop tiny
5 large potatoes: grate (do not peel)
1 cauliflower: chop into small florets
1 broccoli: chop small
juice of 1 lemon

powder spices
    1/4 teaspoon cardamom
    2 heaping teaspoons cayenne
    1 teaspoon cinnamon
    1/2 teaspoon cloves
    4 heaping teaspoons coriander
    1 heaping teaspoon cumin

seed spices
    1/4 teaspoon cumin
    1/4 teaspoon fenugreek
    1/4 teaspoon black mustard

1 teaspoon fennel
2 teaspoons garlic
1/4 teaspoon ginger
1 heaping teaspoon turmeric

Heat 1/4 inch of oil in a large frying pan. Add onion and chilies. Simmer awhile and add the seed spices. Simmer till onions turn clear.

Add the cabbage and potatoes. Mix well. Add cauliflower, 2 teaspoons salt, and a little water to keep the ingredients from sticking. Sprinkle in powder spices and mix well. Add the broccoli. Cover and let simmer, stirring occasionally.

Thirty minutes from the starting time, mix in the lemon juice. Finished. Makes 15 medium servings.

Cooking and the grace of eating together have been important parts of the tradition that descends through Rumi. One can visit his cook's tomb in Konya. When transformation reaches a certain point, one goes into the kitchen to help fix food for the long table. Bawa Muhaiyaddeen improvised this meal on December 17, 1978.

SUNDAY VEGETABLE CURRY

4 cups lentils
4 cups yellow split peas
4 cups green split peas
1 large onion: chop
1 bunch of leeks: slice thin
4 bell peppers: chop
20 unpeeled medium potatoes: quarter lengthwise and cut into 1/4 inch slices.
1 red cabbage: chop small
1/2 regular cabbage: chop small
1 bunch celery: chop into 1/4 inch wide slices
2 bunches watercress: chop
1 bunch broccoli: chop
7 large carrots: grate
3 pounds spinach: chop
juice of 3 lemons

powder spices

1/2 tablespoon cardamom
2 tablespoons cayenne
1 tablespoon cinnamon

seed spices

1/2 teaspoon cumin
1/4 teaspoon fennel
1/2 teaspoon fenugreek

1/2 tablespoon cloves
2 very heaping tablespoons
   coriander
1 very heaping tablespoon cumin
1 tablespoon fennel
3 tablespoons garlic
1 tablespoon ginger
2 tablespoons onion
1/2 tablespoon black pepper
1 heaping tablespoon turmeric

1/2 teaspoon black mustard
10-inch stick cinnamon,
   broken up

Use two separate pots, a skillet, and another 5-gallon main pot.

In one pot cook lentils in a minimum of water till just soft, about 45 minutes. Set aside without draining.

In another pot cook the yellow and green split peas till just soft, about 45 minutes. Set aside without draining.

In the 5-gallon pot heat 1/4 inch of oil. Add the seed spices and cinnamon sticks. When the seeds pop, add the onion and the leeks. Mix the powder spices separately in hot water, making a thin gravy.

When the onions turn clear, add the peppers, the potatoes, and the cabbage. Add the spice gravy with 2 cups of hot rinse water. Add the celery, watercress, 1/4 of the carrots, and the broccoli. Mix the vegetables from top to bottom, then add the spinach, if it will all fit. Sprinkle 6 tablespoons of salt over the top.

In a large skillet, cover the bottom with oil. Heat and add the carrots and any leftover spinach, with 1 tablespoon of salt.

Simmer till just done. Add to main pot.

Fifty minutes from the starting point, mix in the lentils, the split peas, and the lemon juice. Finished. Five gallons, and rice, serves about 60, with enough to carry some home for those who couldn't be there.

RASSUM
   (literally, "pepper water," a spicy broth)

   3 long red or green chili peppers, sliced small
   3 large onions, diced small
   5 cloves of garlic, chopped small
   3 ounces instant concentrated tamarind paste
   Large grocery bag half-full of fresh cherry and Italian tomatoes,
   chopped small (or equivalent amount of regular tomatoes or canned
   pureed tomatoes)

powder spices	seed spices

powder spices
- *1 heaping tablespoon cayenne pepper*
- *1/4 heaping tablespoon cinnamon*
- *1/4 heaping tablespoon cloves*
- *2 very heaping tablespoons coriander*
- *3/4 tablespoon cumin*
- *3/4 tablespoon garlic*
- *1 tablespoon onion*
- *1/2 tablespoon black pepper*
- *1/4 heaping tablespoon turmeric*
- *1 inch peeled and chopped ginger*

seed spices
- *1/2 teaspoon cumin*
- *1/2 teaspoon fennel*
- *1/2 teaspoon fenugreek*
- *1/2 teaspoon black mustard*
- *4-inch stick of cinnamon*

In the largest soup pot you have (4-gallon is not too small), add 1 gallon of hot water or bean stock, the powder spices, and cinnamon stick. Cook for 10 minutes, then add the ginger and half of the onions. Cook another 15 minutes and add the tomatoes. Cook for 25 minutes, stirring occasionally. Meanwhile heat 1/4 inch of oil in a heavy frying pan. Add seed spices. When they just begin to pop and turn light brown (don't let them get too dark), add the chilies, the rest of the onions, and a small amount of broth. Simmer 15 minutes. Add the mix from the frying pan to the soup pot and cook over medium heat for half an hour. Salt to taste. Add 3 ounces of instant concentrated tamarind paste, which can be found in Indian grocery stores. Mix this paste in until it dissolves. This soup is great for using up the extra summer tomatoes. It can be frozen and brought out during the winter whenever a cold threatens. It's a very healing soup. This amount might be enough for 75 to 100 people.

Early Morning Curry and Sunday Vegetable Curry are from Bawa Muhaiyaddeen's *Tasty Economical Cookbook,* vol. 2, available from The Fellowship Press, 5820 Overbrook Ave., Philadelphia, PA 19131. The *Rassum* recipe is courtesy of Sally Green, who watched Bawa fix it and jotted down notes.

↗ References

The numbers for the quatrains and the odes (a pound sign followed by a number) refer to the numbering in Furuzanfar's edition of *Kulliyat-e Shams*, 8 vols. (Teheran: Amir Kabir Press, 1957–1966). The *Mathnawi* references (a roman numeral, I–VI, followed by line numbers) are to Reynold Nicholson's edition (London: Luzac, 1925–1940). The page references to Arberry are to A. J. Arberry's translation, *The Rubaiyat of Jalal al-din Rumi* (London: Emery Walker, 1949).

CHAPTER 1. THE TAVERN

"Who Says Words with My Mouth?" from *Safa Anthology;* "We have a huge barrel of wine . . . ," #1319; "A Community of the Spirit," #2577; "There's a strange frenzy in my head . . . ," #747; "Drunks fear the police . . . ," #731; "A Children's Game," I, 3426–54; "Gone, inner and outer . . . ," #1159; "The wine we really drink . . . ," #1301; "The Many Wines," IV, 2683–96; "Special Plates," #1910; "Burnt Kabob," #2738; "The New Rule," #1861; "This that is tormented . . . ," #190.

CHAPTER 2. BEWILDERMENT

"I Have Five Things to Say," III, 4694–4734; "Acts of Helplessness," II, 1680–1708; "Saladin's Begging Bowl," #1397; "Late, by myself . . . ," #12; "Does sunset sometimes look . . . ," #551; "Be Melting Snow," #2172; "The Fragile Vial," V, 1884–1920, 1959–64; "Where Are We?" VI, 3288–95, 3306–22; "The Friend comes into my body . . . ," #167; "There is a light seed grain . . . ," #667; "Do you think I know . . . ," #1359.

CHAPTER 3. EMPTINESS AND SILENCE

"The Reed Flute's Song," I, 1–18; "A Thirsty Fish," #1823; "Enough Words?" #2155; "This World Which Is Made of Our Love for Emptiness," #950; "Quietness," #636; "Sanai," #996; "A Just-Finishing Candle," V,

672–82; "Craftsmanship and Emptiness," VI, 1369–1420; "Emptiness," I, 1480–1514; "When you are with everyone but me . . . ," #1793; "No Flag," #2449; "The Food Sack," III, 3014–30; "The Night Air," VI, 4876–4916; "Only Breath," from a translation quoted in Pir Vilayat Khan's *The Message in Our Time* (New York: Harper & Row, 1978), 426; "There is a way between voice . . . ," #337.

CHAPTER 4. SPRING GIDDINESS

"Spring," #211; "Where Everything Is Music," #110; "A Great Wagon," #171; "Today, like every other day . . . ," #82; "Out beyond ideas of wrong-doing . . . ," #158; "The breeze at dawn . . . ," #91; "I would love to kiss you . . . ," #388; "Daylight, full of small dancing particles . . . ," #556; "They try to say what you are . . . ," #558; "Come to the orchard in Spring . . . ," #914; "Spring Is Christ," #2003; "Shreds of Steam," #3438; "The Steambath," #809; "The Ground Cries Out," #3048; "Unfold Your Own Myth," #598; "Not a Day on Any Calendar," #2728; "Flutes for Dancing," #2967; "The Shape of My Tongue," #1486; "The Grasses," I, 3325–43; "The Sheikh Who Played with Children," II, 2338–42, 2384–85, 2400–2430, 2436–38, 2442; "Let the lover be disgraceful . . . ," #55; "All day and night, music . . . ," #7.

CHAPTER 5. FEELING SEPARATION

"Sometimes I Forget Completely," #2537; "A Man and a Woman Arguing," I, 2252–2364, 2372–74; "A night full of talking that hurts . . . ," #170; "An Empty Garlic," #2776; "The Diver's Clothes Lying Empty," #2693; "Red Shirt," #1924; "My Worst Habit," #2779; "Don't let your throat tighten . . . ," #825; "Dissolver of Sugar," #3019; "Pale sunlight . . . ," Arberry, 153b.

CHAPTER 6. CONTROLLING THE DESIRE-BODY

"Sexual Urgency . . . ," V, 3831–4034; "Tattooing in Qazwin," I, 2981–3021; "The Center of the Fire," #1304; "Someone who goes with half a loaf . . . ," #494; "The mystery does not get clearer . . . ," #1088; "Muhammad and the Huge Eater," V, 1–149, 163, 167; "Fasting," #1739; "*Bismillah*," #1073; "Wean Yourself," III, 49–62; "After the Meditation," II, 194–223, 260–63; "The Dog in the Doorway," V, 2922–28, 2940–43, 2956–62; "The light you give off . . . ," #2; "Tending Two Shops," II, 590–93, 602–13; "Think that you're gliding out . . . ," #1078.

CHAPTER 7. *SOHBET*

"Talking in the Night," #1335; "Talking Through the Door," #436; "A Mouse and a Frog," VI, 2632, 2665–69, 2681–84; "The Long String," VI, 2686–2786; "The Force of Friendship," VI, 2922–73; "The Vigil," #258; "Two Friends," I, 3065–3101; "The Servant Who Loved His Prayers," III,

3055–76; "Imra'u 'l-Qays," VI, 3986–4010; "All Rivers at Once," #1126; "The Blocked Road," #1837; "A Babbling Child," #2083; "Who sees inside from outside? . . . ," #497; "Constant Conversation," end of #7; "Bonfire at Midnight," #2110; "In Between Stories," VI, 2252–77; "The Question," V, 420–55; "The Music," I, 2084–85; "I saw you last night in the gathering . . . ," #1035; "The Tent," #1051; "Friend, our closeness is this . . . ," #25; "Listen to presences . . . ," #730.

CHAPTER 8. BEING A LOVER

"The Sunrise Ruby," V, 2020–49; "Water from Your Spring," #1001; "You Sweep the Floor," #3050; "Each Note," #532; "Granite and Wineglass," #2357; "Buoyancy," #940; "Music Master," #1195; "When I am with you . . . ," #36; "The minute I heard my first love story . . . ," #1246; "We are the mirror as well as the face . . . ," #1652; "I want to hold you close . . . ," #1080; "Someone Digging in the Ground," #617; "The Phrasing Must Change," I, 4020–43; "The Guest House," V, 3644–46, 3676–80, 3693–95.

CHAPTER 9. THE PICKAXE

"Who Makes These Changes?" VI, 3682–87; "Why Wine Is Forbidden," IV, 2154–58; "On Resurrection Day," V, 2211–20; "The Dream That Must Be Interpreted," IV, 3654–67, 3628–52; "The Pickaxe," IV, 2540–59; "Zikr," IV, 435–66; "The Core of Masculinity," VI, 1430–45; "I honor those who try . . . ," #828; "Dervish at the Door," VI, 1250–67.

CHAPTER 10. ART AS FLIRTATION WITH SURRENDER

"Omar and the Old Poet," I, 2076, 2086–2101, 2106–9, 2163–66, 2175–2220; "An Egypt That Doesn't Exist," #1754; "Chinese Art and Greek Art," I, 3462–85, 3499; "In your light I learn . . . ," Arberry, 178a; "Drumsound rises on the air . . . ," Arberry, 64a; "Are you jealous of the ocean's generosity? . . . ," Arberry, 7b.

CHAPTER 11. UNION

"Gnats Inside the Wind," III, 4624–33, 4644–59; "Meadowsounds," #3079; "Ayaz and the King's Pearl," V, 4035–64, 4075–79, 4083–4117, 4189–92, 4195–4215; "Put This Design in Your Carpet," V, 3292–99, 3310–24; "Hallaj," #1288; "We Three," #2395; "I am filled with you . . . ," #168.

CHAPTER 12. THE SHEIKH

"Chickpea to Cook," III, 4160–68, 4197–4208; "I Have Such a Teacher," #2015; "Sublime Generosity," #1373; "Like This," #1826; "A Bowl," #2805; "Wax," #1628; "No Room for Form," #1145; "Childhood Friends,"

I, 3150–75, 3192–3227; "The Mouse and the Camel," II, 3436–74; "These gifts from the Friend . . . ," #33; "The Lame Goat," III, 1114–27

CHAPTER 13. RECOGNIZING ELEGANCE

"Father Reason," IV, 3259–70; "A craftsman pulled a reed . . . ," #612; "Humble living does not diminish . . . ," #397; "New Moon, Hilal," VI, 1111–1215; "Body Intelligence," IV, 3678–3703, 3708–10; "The Seed Market," IV, 2611–25.

CHAPTER 14. THE HOWLING NECESSITY

"Love Dogs," III, 189–211; "Cry Out in Your Weakness," II, 1932–60; "The Debtor Sheikh," II, 376–444. "You that come to birth . . . ," Arberry, 189b.

CHAPTER 15. TEACHING STORIES

"Nasuh," V, 2228–2316; "Moses and the Shepherd," II, 1720–96; "Joy at Sudden Disappointment," III, 3204–65; "If the beloved is everywhere . . . ," I, 30; "Story Water," V, 228–36.

CHAPTER 16. ROUGH METAPHORS

"Rough Metaphors," III, 3669–85; "Birdwings," III, 3762–66; "I Come Before Dawn," III, 4587–4600; "Checkmate," IV, 74–109; "An Awkward Comparison," IV, 419–33; "Two Kinds of Intelligence," IV, 1960–68; "Two Ways of Running," V, 2163–2204, 2210; "The Importance of Gourdcrafting," V, 1333–1405; "Breadmaking," VI, 3914–79.

CHAPTER 17. SOLOMON POEMS

"Sheba's Gifts to Solomon," IV, 563–97; "Solomon to Sheba," IV, 653–77; "Sheba's Hesitation," IV, 1082–1113; "Sheba's Throne," IV, 863–89; "Solomon's Crooked Crown," IV, 1901–7, 1913, 1918–19, 1923; "The Far Mosque," IV, 475–86; "A bird delegation came to Solomon . . . ," Arberry, 12b.

CHAPTER 18. THE THREE FISH

"If you want what visible reality . . . ," Arberry, 16a; "Gamble everything . . . ," Arberry, 16b; "In a boat down a fast-running creek . . . ," Arberry, 11b; "The Three Fish," IV, 2203–86; "Send the Chaperones Away," IV, 2061–63, 2065–80; "When I remember your love . . . ," Arberry, 153a; "All our lives we've looked . . . ," Arberry, 94a; "The Gift of Water," I, 2850–70.

CHAPTER 19. JESUS POEMS

"I called through your door . . . ," Arberry, 76a; "Jesus on the Lean Donkey," II, 1858–60, 1878–1929; "What Jesus Runs Away From," III, 2570–98; "Christ is the population . . . ," #1091; "There's Nothing Ahead," #425.

CHAPTER 20. IN BAGHDAD, DREAMING OF CAIRO

"In Baghdad, Dreaming of Cairo . . . ," VI, 4167–4275, 4280, 4302–19, 4324–26; "Dying, Laughing," V, 1242–64; "Human Honesty," III, 650–702; "Dalqak's Message," VI, 2510–54; "The Cat and the Meat," V, 3409–29; "Sheikh Kharraqani . . . ," VI, 2019–2190; "The Snake-Catcher . . . ," III, 976–77, 993–1007, 1029–67; "Polishing the Mirror," II, 2059, 2061, 2068–94; "Ali in Battle," I, 3721–50, 3764–71, 3773–82, 3787–89, 3796–98, 3825–30, 3832, 3841, 3844.

CHAPTER 21. BEGINNING AND END

"The King and the Handmaiden and the Doctor," I, 34–205, 215–45; "The Three Brothers and the Chinese Princess," VI, 3583–85, 3630–39, 3654–58, 3699–3706, 3760–69, 3778–84, 3786–92, 3797–98, 3887–3900, 3980–81, 4055–71, 4390–4401, 4410–22, 4589–4604, 4615–31, 4634–53, 4759–93, 4865–76.

CHAPTER 22. GREEN EARS EVERYWHERE

"I used to be shy . . . ," Arberry, 145b; "Green Ears," IV, 3242–3347; "Birdsong brings relief . . . ," Arberry, 169b; "The way of love is not . . . ," Arberry, 37b; "Let your throat-song . . . ," Arberry, 66a; "I have phrases and whole pages . . . ," Arberry, 116a; "You've so distracted me . . . ," Arberry, 140b; "I'm Not Saying This Right," #2166; "The Least Figure," #1538; "I reach for a piece of wood . . . ," #831.

CHAPTER 23. BEING WOVEN

"Of Being Woven," VI, 507–13, 517–25; "The Waterwheel," #393; "The Granary Floor," II, 156–93; "A Song About a Donkey," II, 512–76; "Elephant in the Dark," III, 1259–69.

CHAPTER 24. WISHED-FOR SONG

"A Wished-for Song," #2196; "A Basket of Fresh Bread," V, 1051–94; "When We Pray Alone," VI, 118–28; "One Who Wraps Himself," IV, 1353–1463; "Deliberation," III, 3494–3516; "The Private Banquet," IV, 3755–85; "We are the night ocean . . . ," #1299; "Which is worth more, a crowd . . . ," Arberry, 108b.

CHAPTER 25. MAJESTY

"This We Have Now," I, 1803–13; "The Visions of Daquqi," III, 1972–2029, 2046–83; "The Worm's Waking," IV, 2537–39; "The Freshness," #1047; "Judge a Moth . . . ," #2627; "The morning wind spreads . . . ," #751; "Slave, be aware . . . ," Arberry, 19a.

CHAPTER 26. EVOLUTIONARY INTELLIGENCE

"A Dove in the Eaves," #543; "We have this way of talking . . . ," #403; "This piece of food . . . ," #79; "In the slaughterhouse of love . . . ," #681; "The Witness, the Darling," VI, 2861–83; "In the Arc of Your Mallet," #2195; "Unmarked Boxes," #1937; "The Milk of Millennia," VI, 216–27; "The *You* Pronoun," Prose Preface to Book II; "Birdsong from Inside the Egg," III, 4664–93; "Say I Am You," from a translation quoted in Rudolf Otto's *Mysticism East and West* (New York: Meridian Books, 1957), 93.

CHAPTER 27. THE TURN

"Inside water, a waterwheel . . . ," #723; "You have said what you are . . . ," #394; "A secret turning in us . . . ," #567; "This moment this love comes to rest . . . ," #569; "Keep walking, though there's no place . . . ," #317; "Walk to the well . . . ," #318; "I circle your nest . . . ," #171; "No better love than love . . . ," #152; "Some nights stay up . . . ," #88; "I am so small . . . ," #798; "When you feel your lips . . . ," #807; "The sun is love . . . ," #823; "Something opens our wings . . . ," #1084; "Held like this . . . ," #1125; "I stand up, and this one of me . . . ," #1138; "I have lived on the lip . . . ," #1249; "Real value comes with madness . . . ," Arberry, 36a; "Dance, when you're broken open . . . ," III, 95–97.